The Battle of Chickamauga

Civil War Series

Text by William G. Robertson

Maps by George Skoch

Thanks to James H. Ogden III, Bobby Housch and the interpretive staff at Chickamauga and Chattanooga National Military Park.

Second Printing:1997

Eastern National provides quality educational products and services to America's national parks and other public trusts.

Front cover: The Rock of Chickamauga by Dale Gallon, courtesy of Lower Marsh Creek Press, Gettysburg, PA 17325.

Back Cover: Detail from *The Battle of Chickamauga* by James Walker, courtesy of U.S. Army Historical Collection.

Printed on recycled paper.

National Parks Civil War Series

The Battle of Chickamauga

Of all of the armies that fought in the American Civil War, none struggled in more scenic or more rugged territory than did the Federal Army of the Cumberland and the Confederate Army of Tennessee. Second only in size to their counterparts in the eastern theater, these two armies contended for mastery of the vast area encompassing eastern Tennessee and northern Georgia and Alabama. Separated from their respective capitals by the Appalachian Mountains, the armies shared many characteristics. Both were almost exclusively composed of Americans from the trans-Appalachian region. Both quickly learned that the region's formidable rivers and mountain ranges tended to hinder rather than facilitate offensive movements. Both armies found logistical sustainment difficult in the sparsely settled region, and both depended upon fragile single-track railroads for their lifeblood. All of these difficulties were compounded by the inability of the armies' commanders to make their needs adequately understood in Washington and Richmond. Thus the Army of the Cumberland and the Army of Tennessee labored in relative obscurity. Nevertheless, their struggle was critical to the outcome of the Civil War.

The arena in which the two armies maneuvered was diverse in topography yet rich in resources and strategic potential. Beginning in the rolling farmland around Nashville, Tennessee, the theater stretched east and south toward the foothills, then the main ridges of the Appalachian Mountains. Coursing southwestward through these mountains was the broad Tennessee River, which reached northeastern Alabama before breaching the mountain wall on its way to the Ohio. Nestled on the south bank of the river in the midst of the mountains was the city of Chattanooga, Tennessee, home to some 2,500 people and a growing commercial center. The river brought some of this commerce to Chattanooga, but the city's

Confederate battle line in the woods of Chickamauga. (BL)

primary link to the outside world was the railroad. Four major rail lines entered the city, connecting it with Memphis, Nashville, Richmond, and Atlanta. These railroads both enriched Chattanooga and made it a military objective.

Several factors made retention of the region a matter of the greatest importance to the Confederacy. First, the resources found within it were vital to the new nation's war-making potential. The fertile land southeast of Nashville provided great quantities of food and animals to sustain the basic needs of the Army of Tennessee. In the mountains themselves, numerous caves provided significant amounts of niter, a critical ingredient in gunpowder. Similarly, mines in the vicinity of Ducktown, Tennessee, produced 90 percent of the Confederacy's copper, raw material for percussion caps and artillery projectiles. Second, in strategic terms the region served as a shield protecting the Confederacy's industrial and agricultural heartland in Alabama and Georgia. Taken together, the multiple mountain ranges and the Tennessee River represented a series of physical obstacles that, if used intelligently, could deny enemy access to the Confederacy's vitals for years, if not forever.

For the Union, too, this theater of war was critical to national success. Because southeastern Tennessee provided food, fodder, and animals to sustain the Army of Tennessee, the Union needed to deny it to the Confederacy. Because the mineral resources of the southern mountains contributed mightily to the Confederate war effort, those resources had to be wrested from Richmond's grasp as soon as possible. If the heartland of the Confederacy was ever to be pierced, the combined barrier of Tennessee River and Appalachian Mountains had to be breached. Finally, and this reason loomed large in the thinking of Abraham Lincoln's government, thousands of citizens in eastern Tennessee, northern Georgia, and northeastern Alabama remained loyal to the Union and suffered persecution for that loyalty. Thus the North desired to regain control of the region to reduce the Confederacy's war-making capacity, to facilitate further conquests, and to free masses of people believed to be held against their will.

The Union's objectives for military operations in southeastern Tennessee were articulated as early as October 24, 1862, when Major General William Starke Rosecrans replaced Major General Don Carlos Buell as commander of the new Department of the Cumberland. Rosecrans's instructions from General in Chief Henry Halleck were: "First, to drive the enemy from Kentucky and Middle Tennessee; second, to take and hold East Tennessee, cutting the line of railroad at Chattanooga, Cleveland, or Athens, so as to destroy the connection of the valley of Virginia with Georgia and the other Southern States." The Lincoln administration hoped that Rosecrans could make significant progress before the end of 1862, but it recognized that the road to Chattanooga would be long and difficult. In response to the government's directive, Rosecrans in late December began an offensive movement southeast of Nashville.

MAJOR GENERAL WILLIAM STARKE ROSECRANS

(BL)

Even Rosecrans's enemies agreed he was intellectually brilliant, articulate in speech, firm in his convictions, and physically courageous. He was also a man of prodigious energy, who drove both himself and his subordinates unmercifully.

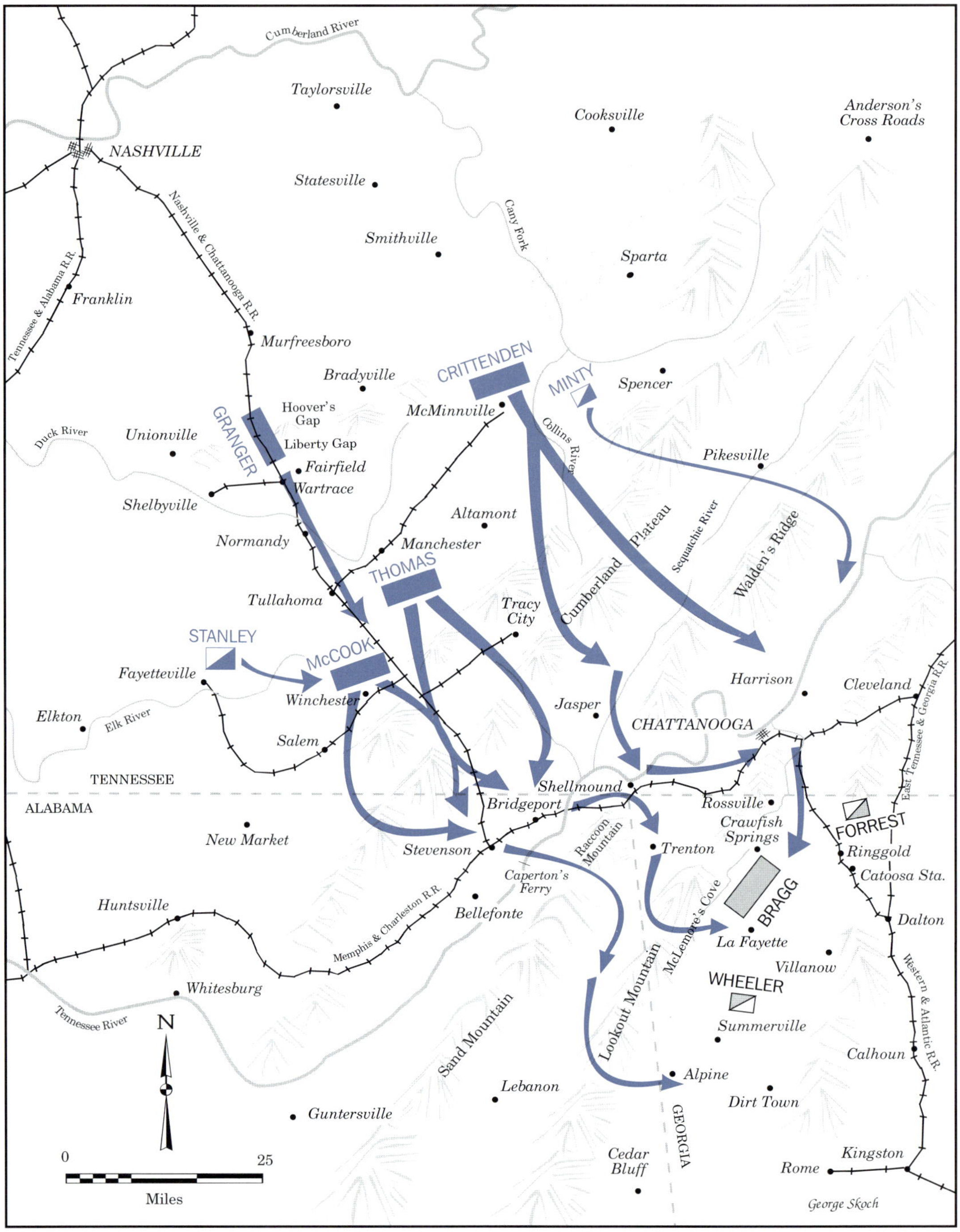

AUGUST 16 TO SEPTEMBER 12, 1863

By mid August, Rosecrans was ready to move from middle Tennessee. His plan called for one corps to feint north of Chattanooga while three others crossed the Tennessee River to the west and south, crossed the Sand and Lookout Mountain ranges, and threatened Bragg's railroad supply line southward. Rosecrans hoped this would trap Bragg or cause him to abandon Chattanooga and retreat into Georgia.

Rosecrans's army began crossing the Cumberland Plateau on August 16 and moved to the river. On August 29, Thomas's, McCook's, and Stanley's corps crossed the river near Stevenson, Bridgeport, and Shellmound. In early September, they moved over the mountains twenty and forty miles south of Chattanooga. Learning of the threat to his rear, Bragg abandoned Chattanooga on September 8. The next day, Federals occupied the city.

As Bragg retreated through LaFayette, he learned of the dispersion of Rosecrans's force and turned to attack in McLemore's Cove. Command dissension made the effort unsuccessful. Rosecrans then began to consolidate his army.

That advance culminated in a bloody fight at Stones River near Murfreesboro, Tennessee. By the end of the battle on January 3, 1863, the Army of Tennessee was in retreat.

The victory at Stones River made Rosecrans famous. Born in Ohio in 1819, he was an 1842 graduate of the United States Military Academy, ranking fifth in a class of fifty-six. Finding promotion slow in the peacetime army and having no opportunity to gain laurels in the Mexican-American War, Rosecrans had resigned his commission in 1854. Life as a businessman/inventor provided little more satisfaction and nearly killed him when a failed experiment severely burned his face. When the Civil War offered Rosecrans an opportunity to return to the military profession, he seized it eagerly, rising to brigadier general by the summer of 1861. Success in western Virginia soon brought transfer to the West, where he gained a semi-independent command under Ulysses Grant. In northern Mississippi Rosecrans fought strongly at the battles of Iuka and Corinth, although he incurred Grant's enmity at the same time. Promoted to major general in September 1862, he lobbied successfully to have the commission backdated to March. Now he commanded one of the nation's three largest field armies.

Even Rosecrans's enemies agreed he was intellectually brilliant, articulate in speech, firm in his convictions, and physically courageous. He was also a man of prodigious energy, who drove both himself and his subordinates unmercifully. A devout Roman Catholic, he retained a personal chaplain on his staff. Unfortunately, these favorable characteristics were balanced by others less beneficial. In temperament Rosecrans tended to be nervous and excitable. He was often impatient and critical of others, especially his superiors, being "short of temper and long of tongue." Neither introspective nor an astute judge of others, Rosecrans was remarkably simple of outlook. Once convinced of the correctness of his views, he was self-righteous in the extreme. Generally affable with his staff, he often immersed himself in details better left to subordinates. This tendency, coupled with his love of philosophical discussion, led him to remain active well past midnight. Unable to sleep late on campaign, but unwilling to modify his nocturnal habits, Rosecrans became increasingly nervous and irascible as the tempo of operations accelerated.

Brigadier General James Abram Garfield

(LC)

Immediately after his victory at Stones River Rosecrans began to rebuild his army. In that battle the army had lost more than 13,000 men and expended large quantities of supplies and equipment. Before any further advance, those losses had to be restored. In addition, casualties among senior leaders necessitated the integration of replacements into the command structure. Rosecrans's own chief of staff, Julius Garesche, had been killed at his side, a void that would be only partially filled by the arrival of Brigadier General James Garfield as Garesche's successor. In addition, the army's cavalry force required

Painting of Zachary Taylor's headquarters near Monterrey, Mexico, 1847. Captain Braxton Bragg is standing in the rear without a hat.

(Courtesy of Smithsonian Institution)

massive expansion. Further, if the army were to advance beyond the fertile fields of Middle Tennessee, enormous quantities of supplies had to be accumulated at Nashville and Murfreesboro. Finally, the army's movements must be coordinated with those of Major General Ambrose Burnside's Army of the Ohio to the northeast and Major General Ulysses Grant's Army of the Tennessee to the west. Despite a stream of complaints from the Lincoln administration, Rosecrans refused to be hurried.

Facing Rosecrans's army was its old nemesis from Perryville and Stones River, the Army of Tennessee, commanded by General Braxton Bragg. Born in North Carolina in 1817, Bragg too was a product of the United States Military Academy, graduating fifth in the class of 1837. Unlike Rosecrans, his pre–Civil War years had been punctuated by combat in the Seminole and Mexican-American wars. In the latter struggle he had attained momentary fame as an artillery battery commander in the Battle of Buena Vista. Like Rosecrans, he also tired of the army's peacetime routine and resigned his commission in 1856. Marrying into wealth, Bragg was a gentleman planter in Louisiana until the crisis of 1861 caused him to cast his lot with the Confederacy. Again like Rosecrans, his rise in rank was speedy, culminating in his promotion to full general in April 1862. Two months later he took command of the troops he would rename the Army of Tennessee. Following the abortive invasion of Kentucky, Bragg brought his army back to Murfreesboro. When Rosecrans advanced upon him in late December, Bragg responded with a vigorous attack; when Rosecrans held firm, Bragg retreated.

While Rosecrans was a hero in the North, Bragg had few admirers in the Confederacy. Like his opponent, Bragg was energetic, intellectually able, and a man of unflinching integrity. While Rosecrans's headquarters was noted for whiskey-fueled conviviality, Bragg's headquarters adopted a spartan tone. Bragg led a disciplined life in both public and private affairs, and his subordinates were expected to conform to his strict code of conduct. This emphasis upon discipline made Bragg appear rigid, brusque, and unsociable to all but a few close acquaintances. Trusting no one, Bragg relied little on his staff and immersed himself in administrative trivia. This self-inflicted burden resulted in frequent bouts of dyspepsia and migraine headaches. Although no commander of the Army of Tennessee concerned himself more with his soldiers' welfare, Bragg's men were generally unaware of his feelings and most hated him. Bragg's inability to relate to others and to understand their shortcomings caused him to have the worst command climate in either army. Only President Jefferson Davis, a man much like Bragg, retained confidence in him in the summer of 1863.

When Bragg's army retreated from the battlefield of Stones River, it withdrew no further than the vicinity of Tullahoma, Tennessee, thirty-five miles to the southeast. There it too prepared itself for another round of fighting. With Federal operations against Vicksburg approaching a climax, Bragg was ordered to send part of his army to Mississippi. Forced to adopt a defensive posture with the remainder, he positioned his two infantry corps forward of the Duck River to protect his railhead at Tullahoma. On the left Lieutenant General Leonidas Polk's corps occupied Shelbyville, while on the right Lieutenant General William Hardee centered his corps around the small village of Wartrace on the Nashville and Chattanooga Railroad. Polk's left was screened by a cavalry division commanded by Brigadier General Nathan Bedford Forrest. Major General Joseph Wheeler's cavalry corps performed a similar function on Hardee's right. On June 20 the Army of Tennessee contained an aggregate present of approximately 55,000 officers and men.

General Braxton Bragg

(USAMHI)

In addition to Bragg's army, serious terrain obstacles stood between Rosecrans and Chattanooga. The first hurdle was a range of hills fifteen miles southeast of Murfreesboro, behind which lay the camps of the Confederate army. Next came the Duck and Elk rivers. If these obstacles could be surmounted, the Federals would face the Cumberland Plateau, a mountain range rising to an altitude of 1,800 feet. Beyond the Cumberland Plateau flowed the Tennessee River, a barrier more than 1,200 feet wide. Beyond the Tennessee was a series of ridges, most notably Sand and Lookout mountains, the latter rising to 2,200 feet. In the mountains the roads were few and rough, and the army would find little to eat. Rosecrans therefore would have to rely upon the Nashville and Chattanooga Railroad for sustenance. Even if the Confederates could be expelled from

Although no commander of the Army of Tennessee concerned himself more with his soldiers' welfare, Bragg's men were generally unaware of his feelings and most hated him.

the region, the logistical challenge of supporting the Army of the Cumberland in such inhospitable terrain would tax the abilities of Rosecrans and his staff.

Without losing sight of Chattanooga, Rosecrans divided his campaign plan into segments. First, he would force Bragg and his army out of Middle Tennessee, into the mountains and possibly beyond the Tennessee River. Second, he would consolidate the ground won and stockpile supplies for the subsequent mountain operations. Third, he would force a crossing of the Tennessee River, a task in which neither the river nor Bragg could be expected to cooperate. Finally, he would advance through the mountains beyond the river, in hopes of either flanking the Army of Tennessee out of Chattanooga or precipitating a major battle. To implement this ambitious plan, the Army of the Cumberland had an aggregate strength of 97,000 officers and men, although garrison details reduced the field force considerably. The army was divided into four infantry corps: the Fourteenth, under Major General George Thomas; the Twentieth, under Major General Alexander McCook; the Twenty-first, under Major General Thomas Crittenden; and the Reserve Corps, under Major General Gordon Granger. Assisting the infantry was a Cavalry Corps, under Major General David Stanley.

Rosecrans's primary objective was to drive Bragg from Middle Tennessee through maneuver instead of battle.

Several practical factors influenced the design of Rosecrans's campaign plan. First, logistical considerations required him to operate generally along the line of the railroad, which would have to be repaired as he advanced. Second, even with the railroad, he would have to wait for the corn to ripen, so as to reduce the amount of forage carried for his thousands of animals. Further, Rosecrans wanted to move in conjunction with General Ambrose Burnside's expedition toward Knoxville, Tennessee. Finally, he believed that a premature advance might cause Bragg to withdraw out of reach and detach even more troops for the defense of Vicksburg. A survey of the Confederate dispositions indicated that a frontal assault on Bragg's army would prove far too costly, while an advance on Bragg's left in the open country around Shelbyville would not trap the Army of Tennessee. The final plan therefore called for feinting at Bragg's left while simultaneously turning his right in the more difficult country to the east. Rosecrans's primary objective was to drive Bragg from Middle Tennessee through maneuver instead of battle.

On June 23, 1863, elements of the Reserve Corps and the Cavalry Corps headed toward Shelbyville to attract Bragg's attention to his left. At the same time, the Twenty-first Corps began its long march around Bragg's right flank. The weather

COLONEL JOHN THOMAS WILDER

(LC)

THIS CURRIER & IVES PRINT, *THE BATTLE OF CHICKAMAUGA, GEORGIA*, IS AN EXAMPLE OF NINETEENTH-CENTURY ROMANTICISM OF THIS AND MANY OTHER BATTLES.

(LC)

now turned sour. Torrential rains began on June 24 and continued virtually without intermission for the next seventeen days, ruining the roads. On that day the Twentieth Corps pushed into Liberty Gap, while the Fourteenth Corps attempted to force its way through Hoover's Gap. Although McCook's men gained most of their objective after stiff skirmishing, the greatest success came at Hoover's Gap. There Colonel John Wilder's mounted infantry brigade, armed with the seven-shot Spencer rifle, brushed aside Confederate pickets and seized the entire gap. When Confederate forces counterattacked, Wilder's men easily maintained their position. East of Thomas, Crittenden's corps slogged deeper into the hills over increasingly difficult roads. Rosecrans had expected to take two days to breach the gaps, giving Crittenden ample time to get around Bragg's flank, but Wilder's audacious move and the rain threatened to upset the Federal timetable.

On June 25 Thomas waited at Hoover's Gap while Crittenden continued his march. The next day Thomas resumed his advance toward the town of Manchester. Leaving one brigade at Liberty Gap, McCook started the remainder of his corps westward after Thomas. Eventually learning that his right had been turned, Bragg ordered a retreat. On June 27 Thomas captured Manchester, but neither McCook nor Crittenden was able to join him because of the poor condition of the roads. On Rosecrans's right Stanley's cavalry drove Wheeler's Confederates from Shelbyville. By that time both of Bragg's infantry corps were already moving southward toward Tullahoma. In an effort to discover Bragg's intent, Rosecrans on June 28 sent Thomas to threaten Tullahoma while McCook, Crittenden, and Stanley concentrated at Manchester. At the same time Wilder's brigade raided across the Elk River to strike the railroad in Bragg's rear at Decherd, Tennessee. As Bragg's army entered the fortifications of Tullahoma, Wilder's men reached the railroad and inflicted some damage before being driven away.

As the Army of the Cumberland approached Tullahoma, Bragg ordered his army to stand fast, but on June 30 he changed his mind. The incessant rain had begun to swell the Elk River in Bragg's rear, threatening his ability to retreat. That evening the Army of Tennessee quietly evacuated its base. On July 1 Federal scouts probing Tullahoma's defenses found them vacant. Learning that Bragg's army was in full retreat, Rosecrans ordered Thomas and McCook to fix the Confederates in position, while Crittenden and Stanley made another flank march to the east. Bragg's lead was too great, however, and by noon the Army of Tennessee was safely beyond the raging Elk River. Rosecrans now slowed the pursuit, preferring to let Bragg go rather than corner him. Only too willing to oblige, Bragg ordered his army to withdraw all the way to Chattanooga. As Bragg's soldiers struggled over the mountains, Rosecrans's men crossed the Elk River and occupied the towns of Decherd, Winchester, and Cowan at the foot of the Cumberland Plateau. At a cost of only 560 Federal casualties, Rosecrans had successfully concluded the first phase of his campaign for Chattanooga.

JOSEPH WHEELER, A MAJOR GENERAL AT CHICKAMAUGA, COMMANDED ONE OF BRAGG'S TWO CAVALRY CORPS.

(BL)

Amid a crescendo of criticism from soldiers and civilians alike, Bragg's dispirited army established defensive positions around Chattanooga in early July. The operations just ended had shown the Army of Tennessee to be a balky machine. Polk and Hardee seemed united only in their dislike for their chief. Wheeler's cavalry had furnished Bragg bad intelligence of Federal movements, then had almost been destroyed at Shelbyville. Quantities of supplies and some irreplaceable heavy ordnance had been abandoned. Nevertheless, the army had retreated in good order, if not in good spirits, and remained willing to contest the line of the Tennessee River.

Bragg deployed Polk's corps in the vicinity of Chattanooga, with one brigade left on the Tennessee's north bank at Bridgeport, Alabama, to provide early warning of Federal intentions. Hardee's corps meanwhile was sent northwest of the city to guard against a Federal thrust across the river between Chattanooga and Knoxville. All told, Bragg's army contained approximately 52,000 officers and men by the end of July.

In a belated attempt to unify its efforts in East Tennessee, the Confederate government on July 25 merged Major General Simon Buckner's Department of East Tennessee into Bragg's Department of Tennessee. Buckner's force added 17,800 troops to Bragg's command, but it also expanded his area of concern northward to the Knoxville area. This administrative action further degraded the command climate within Bragg's department by bringing another enemy into the command structure. Polk and Hardee already had little or no respect for Bragg and were supported in their attitude by many of their principal subordinates. Buckner's animosity toward Bragg stemmed from the unsuccessful invasion of his native Kentucky in 1862, as well as the manner in which his department had been abolished. The increased friction represented by Buckner's arrival was momentarily mitigated by the departure on July 14 of Hardee, who was transferred to Mississippi at his own request. Hardee's replacement was Lieutenant General Daniel Harvey Hill, a North Carolinian who had served with Bragg in Mexico.

In early August the War Department asked Bragg if he could take the offensive given significant reinforcements from Mississippi. Bragg responded that the geo-

THE ARMY OF THE CUMBERLAND'S SUPPLIES ARRIVED BY RAIL TO STEVENSON, ALABAMA, AND FROM HERE WERE TRANSPORTED BY WAGON. THE ARTIST WAS LOOKING TO THE NORTHWEST IN THIS VIEW OF STEVENSON.

(LC)

graphical obstacles, his tenuous logistical situation, and his weakness precluded an advance into or beyond the mountains. If the Federals incautiously passed those barriers, however, he believed that the time would be right for a counterstroke. Bragg therefore contented himself with restoring discipline to his army, apprehending deserters, and conserving his own increasingly shaky health. Believing that the mountains and the Tennessee River were sufficient to shield his front, he withdrew the brigade from Bridgeport, leaving the territory beyond the river to Rosecrans. Keeping his two infantry corps concentrated around Chattanooga, he relied upon his cavalry to guard his flanks. Forrest's command covered the army's right, extending northwest until it met Buckner's pickets near Knoxville. Wheeler was responsible for the security of the army's left as far as northern Alabama. While Forrest patrolled actively, Wheeler permitted the bulk of his command to rest and refit far south of the Tennessee.

For six weeks after the Tullahoma operations ended, the Army of the Cumberland remained in its camps at the foot of the Cumberland Plateau. In order to establish a presence in the Tennessee River valley, Rosecrans sent Major General Philip Sheridan's division of McCook's corps to occupy Stevenson and Bridgeport, Alabama. Sheridan followed the line of the railroad, which pierced the mountains in a 2,200-foot tunnel near Cowan, Tennessee, then passed through Stevenson en route to its crossing of the river on a 2,700-foot span at Bridgeport. The bridge had been destroyed by the retreating Confederates, but the tunnel was virtually undamaged. Of more immediate concern to Rosecrans was the state of the railroad between Murfreesboro and Cowan. The large Elk River bridge and several smaller spans had been destroyed, preventing the rapid accumulation of supplies needed to sustain a

MAJOR GENERAL GEORGE HENRY THOMAS

(BL)

High Command Politics

Entering the Chickamauga Campaign, the command structure of the Union forces superficially appeared more unified than that of their opponents. While not a personal confidant of President Abraham Lincoln, Major General William Rosecrans retained the confidence of the chief executive. Rosecrans's victory at Stones River, coming amid Federal disasters elsewhere, gave him considerable credibility with Lincoln. That trust and confidence, however, was not so apparent among Rosecrans, Secretary of War Edwin Stanton, and General in Chief Henry Halleck. Stanton disliked Rosecrans for a variety of reasons, mostly stemming from the clash of strong personalities. Halleck tried to ameliorate the friction, but he too became exasperated with Rosecrans's prickly personality, his willingness to find slights in the gentlest suggestions, and his seemingly interminable delay in beginning the campaign. Nor were Rosecrans's neighboring department commanders, Ulysses Grant and Ambrose Burnside, especially interested in furthering the interests of the Army of the Cumberland. Grant and Rosecrans had clashed over affairs at Iuka and Corinth, while Burnside pursued his own agenda in East Tennessee at Rosecrans's expense. Fully aware of his enemies elsewhere, Rosecrans was oblivious to disloyalty within his own official family. Chief of staff James Garfield, a protégé of Secretary of the Treasury Salmon Chase, secretly showed more loyalty to his patron than to his commander by reporting negatively on Rosecrans's operations. Similarly, Charles Dana, an assistant secretary of war who joined Rosecrans in mid-campaign, was a clandestine conduit to Secretary Stanton for potentially damaging information. Coupled with the fact that corps commanders Alexander McCook and Thomas Crittenden were weak and ineffectual, these fissures within the Union command structure boded ill for Rosecrans if the coming campaign were to be less than successful.

Across the lines, Braxton Bragg presided over an openly fractious command structure. His relations with President Jefferson Davis were excellent, the latter's respect for Bragg dating to the Mexican War. With Secretary of War James Seddon in Davis's shadow and with no Confederate counterpart to the Union's Halleck, Bragg was essentially responsible only to the Confederate president. His difficulties, instead, lay with his subordinates. The senior corps commander of the Army of Tennessee, Lieutenant General Leonidas Polk, was neither militarily proficient nor unequivocally loyal. Worse, he himself was a friend of President Davis and felt free to correspond directly with him on military matters, usually to Bragg's detriment. Seconding Polk was a disaffected contingent of Tennesseans led by Major General Benjamin Cheatham. Joining Bragg's opponents in mid-campaign was Major General Simon Buckner, whose antipathy stemmed from the ill-fated Kentucky Campaign and the fact that his department had been peremptorily subsumed into Bragg's. Nor was Lieutenant General Daniel Harvey Hill a team player, his corrosive personality almost instantly clashing with the army commander's. Finally, the arrival of Lieutenant General James Longstreet, who barely concealed a burning desire to supplant Bragg, contributed greatly to the turmoil swirling about the embattled army commander. The task of molding such a disgruntled collection of subordinates into a cohesive fighting machine during an active campaign would ultimately prove to be beyond Braxton Bragg's capacity.

The task of molding such a disgruntled collection of subordinates into a cohesive fighting machine during an active campaign would ultimately prove to be beyond Braxton Bragg's capacity.

Major General Simon Bolivar Buckner was one of the principal figures in the Confederate fiasco at McLemore's Cove and led the post-Chickamauga anti-Bragg movement.

(LC)

further advance. Rosecrans thus drove his engineers to rebuild the track as fast as possible. Even with the railroad in full operation, the army could not feed its thousands of animals without relying upon local forage. Rosecrans therefore postponed further movement until the corn ripened in the river bottoms.

While his army paused, Rosecrans evaluated his subordinates. He was pleased with chief-of-staff Garfield. Of the corps commanders, Major General George Thomas, 47, was Rosecrans's mainstay, a careful, solid performer. Thomas's

MAJOR GENERAL GORDON GRANGER

(LC)

Fourteenth Corps, 27,000 men in four divisions, was the largest in the army. Major General Alexander McCook, 32, had a more checkered reputation. Although a West Point graduate, his poor performance at Perryville and Stones River had raised serious questions about his maturity and judgment. Ohio political connections kept him in command, but Rosecrans would have to supervise him closely. McCook's Twentieth Corps contained almost 17,000 men in three divisions. Major General Thomas Crittenden, 44, was another weak performer. A Kentuckian, Crittenden lacked McCook's formal military training but was equally well-connected politically. His actions also would have to be closely monitored. Crittenden's Twenty-first Corps numbered 17,000 men in three divisions. Commanding the Reserve Corps was Major General Gordon Granger, 40, a gruff West Pointer lacking experience in large battles. Granger's command contained 20,000 men in three divisions. Finally, Major General David Stanley, 35, commanded the Cavalry Corps, 12,000 men in two divisions.

MAJOR GENERAL THOMAS LEONIDAS CRITTENDEN

(BL)

During the long delay at the foot of the mountains Rosecrans perfected the remaining phases of his campaign plan. The army would move over the Cumberland Plateau into the valley of the Tennessee River, then, after a brief pause to accumulate supplies, cross the river itself. The width of the river precluded an opposed crossing, so a deception operation above Chattanooga would distract Bragg while the army crossed downstream. The plan's final phase consisted of an advance through the mountains on a wide front. Crittenden would threaten Chattanooga from the west, Thomas would strike southeast over Lookout Mountain twenty miles south of the city, while McCook and Stanley would plunge even further to the southeast toward Bragg's railroad to Atlanta. If Bragg did nothing, his supply line would be severed and he would be trapped in Chattanooga. If he

MEMBERS OF WILDER'S UNION BRIGADE OF MOUNTED INFANTRY RIDE PAST A STOCKADE ON THE NASHVILLE AND CHATTANOOGA RAILROAD.

(*SOLDIER IN OUR CIVIL WAR*)

evacuated Chattanooga without a fight, Rosecrans would again have achieved his objective. If Bragg chose to fight, Rosecrans was confident the Army of the Cumberland would gain the victory.

On August 16, 1863, Rosecrans ordered the Army of the Cumberland into motion. The roads that traversed the Cumberland Plateau were poor, making the army's passage extremely difficult. Nevertheless, with the assistance of infantrymen heaving on wheels and ropes, the army and its vehicles entered the Tennessee River valley within a week. Rosecrans's engineers had already placed the railroad in full working order and supplies were rapidly accumulating for the next phase of the plan. In the bottomlands along the river the corn was already beginning to ripen. Confident of success, Rosecrans negotiated contracts with civilian firms to reconstruct the railroad bridge at Bridgeport as well as a large span over Running Water Creek nearer Chattanooga. As the army settled into its temporary camps between the mountains and the river, engineers built platforms to protect the growing dumps around Stevenson and Bridgeport from the elements. Among the items that arrived by rail were pontoons for bridging the river and small disassembled steamboats to ferry supplies to Chattanooga once it was captured.

At the same time that the Army of the Cumberland reached the Tennessee River downstream from Chattanooga, Rosecrans implemented his deception plan north of the city. Under Crittenden's general direction, four brigades began to simulate preparations for a river crossing above Chattanooga. The main role in this effort went to Wilder's mounted infantry brigade. Out of sight of the Confederate pickets, Wilder's men pounded tubs and sawed boards to simulate the building of rafts and boats. The lumber was then cast into the river to float downstream into Confederate territory. In addition, Wilder on August 21 placed Captain Eli Lilly's Eighteenth Indiana Battery on Stringer's Ridge opposite Chattanooga itself and opened fire. Lasting for several days, Lilly's bombardment wrecked Bragg's pontoon train, sank two small steamers, damaged numerous buildings, and caused several civilian casualties.

PAINTING BY WILLIAM TRAVIS OF THE FEDERALS CROSSING THE TENNESSEE RIVER NEAR STEVENSON, ALABAMA. ROSECRANS IS SHOWN ON HORSEBACK, POINTING HIS SWORD.

(COURTESY OF SMITHSONIAN INSTITUTION)

The shelling, coupled with the apparent activity upstream, convinced Bragg that the impending Federal crossing would be above the city.

A week after he initiated the deception plan, Rosecrans ordered the Army of the Cumberland across the Tennessee River in four places. The first crossing came at Caperton's Ferry, four miles from Stevenson, on August 29. There Colonel Hans Heg's brigade of the Twentieth Corps rowed across to secure the opposite shore while engineers of the Pioneer Brigade began constructing a pontoon bridge over the 1,250-foot-wide river. On the evening of August 30, twenty-one river miles upstream, Colonel Edward King's brigade of the Fourteenth Corps opened a second major crossing point at Shellmound, Tennessee. King was soon followed by most of Crittenden's Twenty-first Corps. Lacking a bridge, Crittenden's troops used captured small boats and a large raft built by engineers. The next crossing site was located at the mouth of Battle Creek, Tennessee, six miles below Shellmound. There Brigadier General John Brannan's division of the Fourteenth Corps constructed a makeshift flotilla of dugouts and rafts and sailed them across the stream, beginning on August 31.

Without bridges, neither the Shellmound nor Battle Creek sites could permanently support the army on the south bank of the Tennessee. That role was assumed by the bridge erected at Bridgeport by Sheridan's division. There the river split into two channels as it flowed around Long Island, a wide but relatively shallow channel north of the island and a narrow, deep channel to the south. Sheridan combined the talents of an engineer regiment and some of his own infantrymen to produce a bridge that spanned the 2,700-foot gap in three days. A simple A-frame trestle reached across the shallow channel to Long Island and the army's remaining pontoons extended the bridge across the narrow gap to the south bank. Although the trestle collapsed twice in its first day of operation, causing the loss of some supplies and one mule, it was quickly repaired. The spans at Bridgeport and Caperton's Ferry thus became the conduits for the massive wagon trains that would carry supplies to the advancing units from the supply dumps at Stevenson.

By September 4 virtually all of Rosecrans's army, except for Reserve Corps elements guarding the railroad, had safely crossed the Tennessee River. Confederate opposition had consisted of a few cavalrymen who either fled or were captured. Ahead lay the looming bulk of Sand Mountain, 2,000 feet high. Beyond Sand Mountain the few available roads dropped abruptly into narrow Lookout Valley. Beyond this valley Lookout Mountain rose to 2,200 feet. A plateau like Sand Mountain, Lookout was much narrower than its neighbor. Three rough roads traversed the mountain in the campaign area. At its northern end a rocky road climbed

THE CONFEDERATES DESTROYED THE RAILROAD BRIDGE (BACKGROUND) OVER THE TENNESSEE RIVER AT BRIDGEPORT, ALABAMA, IN THEIR RETREAT FROM MIDDLE TENNESSEE. MAJOR GENERAL PHILIP H. SHERIDAN'S UNION DIVISION CONSTRUCTED THE TRESTLE AND PONTOON BRIDGE (FOREGROUND) IN LATE AUGUST 1863 AS PART OF ROSECRANS'S ADVANCE PRIOR TO CHICKAMAUGA. AN ENGINEERING WEAKNESS CAUSED THE TRESTLE STRUCTURE TO COLLAPSE TWICE DURING THE FEDERAL CROSSINGS. IN THIS PHOTO, THE TEMPORARY BRIDGE IS UNDER CONSTRUCTION FOR THE FIRST TIME.

(MINNESOTA HISTORICAL SOCIETY)

over a spur and entered Chattanooga Valley just south of the city. Twenty miles to the south, an even more primitive track ascended the mountain at Johnson's Crook and descended into Chattanooga Valley at Stevens Gap. Another twenty miles south, a final road climbed Lookout Mountain at Winston's Gap and entered Chattanooga (Broomtown) Valley via Henderson's Gap. Rosecrans intended to use these three tracks to place the Army of the Cumberland behind Bragg's army and force it to react.

In Chattanooga Bragg remained mesmerized by Wilder's demonstrations and reports that Burnside was moving toward Knoxville. Believing that Rosecrans must remain within supporting distance of Burnside, he continued to anticipate a crossing upstream from Chattanooga. A call for reinforcements had netted two divisions of approximately 8,500 men which arrived from Mississippi at the end of August. Deciding that Buckner could not resist Burnside successfully, Bragg ordered the Kentuckian to bring his mobile force nearer Chattanooga. With the troops from Mississippi and Buckner's men Bragg felt reasonably secure behind his river and mountain barrier. That security was shattered on September 1 when a civilian reported a major Federal crossing in the Stevenson-Bridgeport area. During the next few days reports confirming the Federal advance gradually trickled into Bragg's headquarters. By September 6 he was finally ready to evacuate Chattanooga, but Polk and Hill persuaded him to postpone the movement pending more definite information.

THIS PHOTOGRAPH OF MAJOR GENERAL ALEXANDER MCDOWELL MCCOOK AND HIS STAFF WAS TAKEN IN THE SUMMER OF 1863. MCCOOK'S TROOPS WOULD MARCH THE GREATEST DISTANCE OF ANY UNION CORPS TO REACH THE CHICKAMAUGA BATTLEFIELD. (LC)

While Bragg hesitated, Rosecrans resumed his advance. Gathering his divisions at Shellmound, Crittenden pushed eastward through Running Water Canyon into Lookout Valley. There Brigadier General Thomas Wood's division began to probe toward the northern tip of Lookout Mountain. On Crittenden's right, Thomas crossed Sand Mountain, paused briefly near Trenton, Georgia, then headed south toward Johnson's Crook. Still further south, McCook's Twentieth Corps crossed Sand Mountain, then halted around Valley Head, Alabama, to allow Stanley's cavalrymen to pass in front. Climbing Lookout Mountain at Winston's Gap, McCook's leading elements descended to Alpine, Georgia, while the cavalry scouted in front of them. McCook was now twenty airline miles south of Thomas, forty airline miles south of Chattanooga, and little more than thirty airline miles from Bragg's lifeline, the Western and Atlantic Railroad. By road, however, McCook and Stanley were much farther from each of these points.

When he finally learned that Federal units were crossing Lookout Mountain, Bragg on September 7 ordered the evacuation of Chattanooga. On the next day Hill's and Polk's corps took the direct road

CRAWFISH SPRINGS WAS THE LAST SOURCE OF WATER FOR MANY UNION SOLDIERS PRIOR TO THE BATTLE OF CHICKAMAUGA. THE ENTIRE CAMPAIGN WAS MARKED BY A WATER SHORTAGE DUE TO A DROUGHT IN THE SUMMER OF 1863.

(NA)

south toward LaFayette, Georgia. Using a parallel road to the east was Buckner's command and a small Reserve Corps under Major General William Walker. Forrest's cavalrymen provided the army's rear guard, while Wheeler attempted to impede the Federal advance. That night Bragg ordered his army to concentrate around LaFayette. On September 9 Hill took position on Pigeon Mountain, a spur of Lookout, and Polk faced northward toward Chattanooga. Everyone else continued toward LaFayette. That evening, discovering that a Federal force had incautiously entered McLemore's Cove, a small valley bordered by Lookout and Pigeon mountains, Bragg saw a chance to strike a counterblow. At 11:45 P.M. he ordered Hill to attack westward from Pigeon Mountain while Major General Thomas Hindman's division of Polk's corps drove southward in the cove itself.

Probing over Lookout Mountain, Crittenden's leading elements discovered that Chattanooga had been evacuated. They raced into the city and were soon met by the deception force from across the river. Upon learning that Chattanooga had been taken, Rosecrans became ecstatic; the goal of his campaign had been attained without a fight. Still, with the Army of Tennessee in apparently panic-stricken retreat, a vigorous pursuit might destroy Bragg's army. Before ordering such a pursuit, Rosecrans called Thomas to headquarters to arrange the details of the movement. The cautious Thomas quietly but firmly argued that the Army of the Cumberland was too widely dispersed to begin a pursuit. In addition, the army's supply line remained fragile. Thomas therefore recommended that Rosecrans consolidate his position in Chattanooga before resuming the campaign. Influenced by the bloodless capture of Chattanooga, Rosecrans dismissed Thomas's counsel out of hand. The units of the Army of the Cumberland would immediately begin pursuit from wherever they happened to find themselves.

MAJOR GENERAL JAMES S. NEGLEY AND HIS STAFF AT COVE SPRING, ALABAMA, AUGUST 1863.

(LC)

Rosecrans's decision meant that Thomas's leading division, Major General James Negley's, would advance toward LaFayette by way of Dug Gap in Pigeon Mountain. En route, Negley would have to

The Widow Davis House sat at an important junction in McLemore's Cove. This photo was taken circa 1957.

(NPS)

traverse the floor of McLemore's Cove for nearly six miles. At 10:00 A.M. on September 10 he began his march with 4,600 men. Brushing aside Confederate skirmishers, he pressed forward to Davis Cross Roads in sight of Dug Gap. Told of a heavy enemy force approaching his left, Negley nevertheless occupied a position within the mouth of the gap by late afternoon. There he remained until 3:00 A.M. on September 11, when he withdrew to a hillside near Davis Cross Roads. At the same time Brigadier General Absalom Baird's division marched to Negley's assistance. Shortly after Baird's 3,400 troops arrived, Confederate skirmishers drove in Negley's pickets. Sensing danger, Negley ordered Baird to occupy the front line while his own men withdrew. Soon after Baird completed the relief, Confederate pressure forced him to withdraw also. The two divisions then leapfrogged their way back to safety at the foot of Stevens Gap.

Bragg had originally expected Hill to control all offensive movements in the cove. Hill had received the order late and had then found other excuses for not moving. In turn, the normally aggressive Hindman had suddenly become overcautious and advanced too gingerly into the cove. Learning that Hill would not be moving, Bragg sent Buckner's two divisions to Hindman as reinforcements. Instead of stiffening Hindman's resolve, Buckner's presence caused further delay when Hindman convened a council of war. Fearing they were being trapped, the council members called for inaction until the situation was clarified. During the night of September 10–11 Bragg sent explicit orders to Hindman to attack at dawn, but Hindman's courier garbled the message. By the time Hindman finally decided to resume his advance, Negley and Baird had already begun their withdrawal. At all times the Federals in the cove had been outnumbered at least three to one, but Hill, Hindman, and Buckner had proved unable to capitalize on their superiority. Disgusted at the lost opportunity, Bragg ordered his forces out of the cove.

Even as Negley and Baird were escaping Bragg's trap, Rosecrans was issuing additional pursuit orders to his scattered commanders. Gradually, as more evidence of Bragg's aggressive intent reached him, Rosecrans became concerned about the position of his units around Alpine. In peremptory orders on September 12 he ordered McCook and the cavalry to meet Thomas at the foot of Stevens Gap. Only when those segments of the army were united could they move north to join Crittenden near Lee and Gordon's Mill. Rosecrans's order to McCook took a full day to reach Alpine. Ignorant of the road network on Lookout Mountain and informed that McLemore's Cove was not secure, McCook saw no alternative but to retrace his steps over Lookout Mountain. Once back at Valley Head, he could march north and cross Lookout again at Johnson's

McLemore's Cove

Unable to defend the line of the Tennessee River successfully, Braxton Bragg believed his best chance for victory lay in using the mountains around Chattanooga to defeat William Rosecrans's army in detail. Thus, when Federal units crossed Lookout Mountain and threatened his railroad to Atlanta, Bragg evacuated Chattanooga on September 8 and initiated his own campaign of maneuver. Moving southward toward LaFayette, Georgia, Bragg learned that a Federal column was entering McLemore's Cove, a V-shaped valley formed by Lookout Mountain and a spur named Pigeon Mountain. The northern end of the valley was open, and several gaps provided access to the valley from the east. With his army screened by Pigeon Mountain, Bragg saw an opportunity to destroy the Federals in the cove before they could receive assistance. Accordingly, at 11:45 P.M. on September 9, he ordered Lieutenant General Daniel Harvey Hill, whose corps guarded the gaps in Pigeon Mountain, to send a division into the cove toward Davis Cross-Roads. At the same time Major General Thomas Hindman was to enter the cove from the north and also drive toward Davis Cross-Roads. The proposed victim of Bragg's plan was Major General James Negley's division of George Thomas' XIV Corps. Convinced that Bragg was in wild retreat, Rosecrans had pressured Thomas to accelerate his pursuit. Although Negley was twelve hours ahead of Brigadier General Absalom Baird's division, he entered the cove through Stevens Gap on September 9. Negley's orders were to cross the cove, penetrate Dug Gap in Pigeon Mountain, and drive on LaFayette. He began the movement at 10 A.M. on September 10.

While Negley's 4,600 troops marched across the cove, Bragg's plan began to unravel. Receiving his orders late, Harvey Hill uncharacteristically claimed he was unable to participate. In contrast, Hindman moved promptly and by 6 A.M. was only four miles north of Davis Cross-Roads with 6,500 men. Without Hill, Hindman became overcautious and spent the remainder of the day moving only one mile further. Bragg, meanwhile, reinforced Hindman with Major General Simon Buckner's corps. When Buckner arrived at 5 P.M., the normally aggressive Hindman outnumbered Negley three to one, yet he did not resume the advance. Told of the Confederate concentration by friendly citizens, Negley that night withdrew his main body to a defensive position just east of the crossroads. By the next morning, when Hindman resumed his tentative advance, Baird's division had arrived. As Hindman inched forward and some of Hill's men advanced from Pigeon Mountain, Negley replaced his division with Baird's and began a withdrawal to Stevens Gap. Apprised of the Federal retreat, Hindman pushed forward but clashed only briefly with Baird's rear guard. Incensed that his subordinates had bungled an opportunity to cripple Rosecrans's largest corps, Bragg angrily ordered Confederate forces to evacuate McLemore's Cove. Surrendering the initiative to Bragg, Rosecrans now abandoned all thought of pursuit and attempted to concentrate his scattered corps. Although Bragg would try again to defeat the Federals before that concentration could be completed, his best opportunity to do so was lost at McLemore's Cove.

At all times the Federals in the cove had been outnumbered at least three to one, but Hill, Hindman, and Buckner had proved unable to capitalize on their superiority. Disgusted at the lost opportunity, Bragg ordered his forces out of the cove.

Crook and Stevens Gap. This route would require three days to negotiate; until then the Army of the Cumberland would remain in a dangerously dispersed condition.

Back at LaFayette Bragg saw another offensive opportunity when Forrest reported that Federal units were moving across his front. This time the mission went to Polk, whose corps was concentrated near Rock Spring Church north of LaFayette. Polk's orders were simple: attack at dawn on September 13. When morning came without any evidence of battle, Bragg rode to the scene. He found no attack in progress and little evidence of one in preparation. When Polk's skirmishers finally advanced, they found no Federals in their front. Angry at another apparent failure to destroy an exposed portion of the Army of the Cumberland, Bragg returned to LaFayette. Although he believed Polk had irresponsibly squandered an opportunity for victory, in fact none existed on September 13. The Federals detected by Forrest had been the remainder of Crittenden's corps moving from Ringgold to join Wood's division at Lee and Gordon's Mill. By the morning of September 13 Crittenden's concentration at the mill was complete and the fleeting chance for

LEE AND GORDON'S MILL, AT THE CROSSING OF THE CHATTANOOGA-LAFAYETTE ROAD OVER CHICKAMAUGA CREEK, BECAME ONE OF THE PRINCIPAL LANDMARKS OF THE BATTLEFIELD. A POSTWAR MILL STRUCTURE OCCUPIES THIS SITE TODAY. (LC)

Confederate success was gone.

At LaFayette Bragg learned of Federal units at Alpine, twenty miles to the southwest. Coupled with known Federal concentrations in McLemore's Cove and at Lee and Gordon's Mill, these forces could be interpreted as evidence of a massive double envelopment by the Federal army. In reality McCook was scrambling to withdraw from Alpine, while Thomas and Crittenden crouched defensively in their respective enclaves. To Bragg, however, his position appeared precarious. Ever since the evacuation of Chattanooga, Bragg's reserve stocks of food and ammunition had been on railroad cars parked around Resaca, Georgia, more than twenty difficult miles to the east. Those stores needed protection, particularly if the army had to fight a large engagement near LaFayette. With the enemy seemingly closing upon him, with his subordinates unable or unwilling to do his bidding, and with his logistical arrangements extremely tenuous, Bragg could hardly look with equanimity upon the future. The only encouraging news was an unofficial report that troops were arriving in Atlanta from Virginia with orders to reinforce the Army of Tennessee.

For the next four days both armies labored to improve their respective positions. Abandoning the offensive, Rosecrans attempted to consolidate his scattered units, including elements of Granger's Reserve Corps, before withdrawing to Chattanooga. If the Confederates left him alone, he could soon muster a field force of slightly more than 62,000 effectives. At a council of war on September 15 Bragg's corps commanders all agreed that a drive toward Chattanooga offered the best chance for success. In preparation for an advance Bragg relocated his base from Resaca to Catoosa Station near Ringgold. Around 3:00 A.M. on the morning of September 17 he learned officially that Lieutenant General James Longstreet was bringing a large contingent of troops to join him. Often proposed, the transfer of the First Corps of the Army of Northern Virginia to the western theater had finally been authorized by Jefferson Davis on September 6, but Burnside's capture of Knoxville on September 2 had blocked the direct route from Virginia. Longstreet's 12,000 men had been forced to detour over a succession of railroads in the lower South, nearly doubling their transit time. In hopes that more of Longstreet's men would become available for the offensive, Bragg postponed the advance for one day.

On September 17 the last of McCook's corps reached the foot of Stevens Gap, permitting Thomas to begin edging northward toward Crittenden's position. That day Bragg rescheduled his offensive for the morning of September 18. If Longstreet were there by that time, well and good; if not, he could wait no longer. Bragg proposed to move most of the Army of Tennessee northward beyond the Federal left flank at Lee and Gordon's Mill, then cross Chickamauga Creek and drive southward, pushing the Army of the Cumberland back into McLemore's Cove. The final operations order specified four crossings over the Chickamauga, from north to south: Brigadier General Bushrod Johnson's division at Reed's Bridge; Walker's Reserve Corps at Alexander's Bridge or Byram's Ford; Buckner's corps at Thedford's Ford; and Polk's corps at Dalton's Ford. Hill's corps would anchor the army's left, while Forrest and Wheeler covered the army's northern and southern flanks respectively.

LIEUTENANT GENERAL JAMES LONGSTREET

(LC)

On September 17 the Army of Tennessee numbered just under 60,000 effectives, organized in four infantry and two cavalry corps. While the troops were as good as the Confederacy had to offer, their leaders were a mixed bag. Lieutenant General Leonidas Polk, 57, the senior corps commander, was a West Point graduate but had spent virtually his entire life in the Episcopal ministry. A friend of Jefferson Davis but an inveterate opponent of Bragg, Polk tended to obey orders in a maddeningly cavalier fashion. In contrast, Lieutenant General Daniel Harvey Hill, 42, was a professional soldier and a strong fighter. His querulous personality, however, made him a difficult subordinate. Major General Simon Buckner, 40, was sulking over the loss of his department and had retreated into passivity. Among the infantry commanders, only Major General William Walker, 46, the aggressive commander of the newly formed Reserve Corps, seemed to have no animosity against his chief. Dashing Major General Joseph Wheeler, 27, had Bragg's confidence but had repeatedly failed to see beyond romantic saber charges. Dour Brigadier General Nathan Bedford Forrest, 42, perhaps the most competent of all, held both Wheeler and Bragg in contempt. Such men were now about to lead the Army of Tennessee into battle.

BRIGADIER GENERAL NATHAN BEDFORD FORREST

(LC)

Early on the morning of September 18 Brigadier General Bushrod Johnson put his troops into motion. Initially taking the wrong road from Ringgold, he eventually got his command headed west on the Reed's Bridge Road. As he neared an

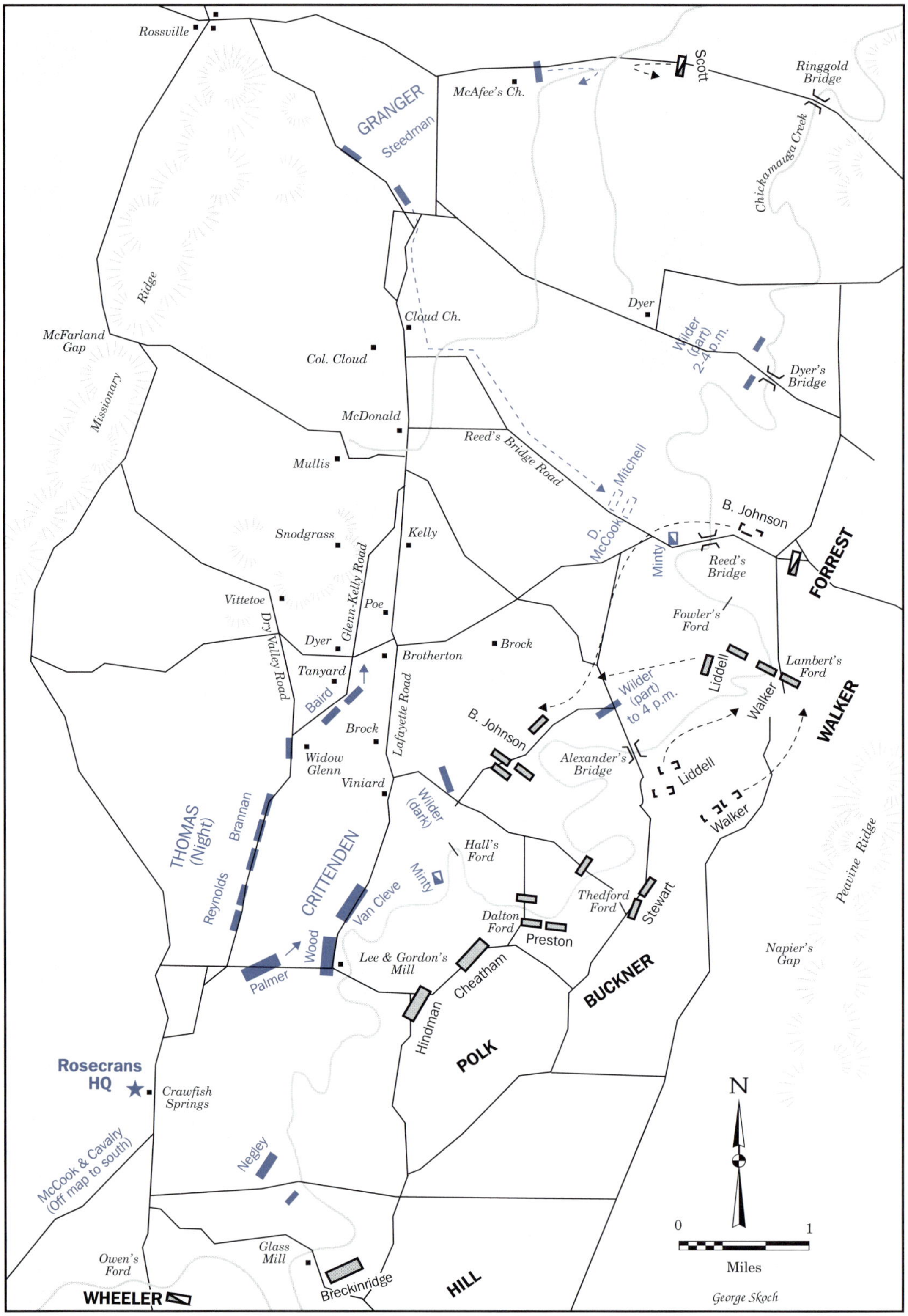

FRIDAY, SEPTEMBER 18, 1863

Bragg failed to count on stiff Union resistance at the Chickamauga crossings of Reed's and Alexander's bridges. At 7:00 A.M., September 18, 1863, at Peavine Creek, Minty's brigade met elements of Bushrod Johnson's division. Minty was slowly forced back to Reed's Bridge by noon. Minty continued to delay until mid-afternoon when elements of Forrest's cavalry corps caused him to withdraw. The Confederates then crossed the bridge and turned south near Jay's steam sawmill, en route toward Lee and Gordon's Mill.

At Alexander's Bridge, at noon, Walker's Reserve Corps met Wilder's brigade, and Eli Lilly's battery. Walker was not able to cross and had to reach the west side of the creek at another point, Lambert's Ford, but not until 4:30.

Bushrod Johnson's approach from the north forced Wilder from Alexander's Bridge. Wilder withdrew in front of Bushrod Johnson and stopped the Confederates short of the Lafayette Road at dark, east of the Viniard Farm. During the night Thomas's corps marched to the Kelly Farm area.

insignificant stream named Peavine Creek, his advance guard encountered Federal cavalry pickets who fired and withdrew to their supports. Johnson had found Colonel Robert Minty's brigade, whose mission was to deny the Reed's Bridge crossing to the Confederates. Outnumbered five to one, Minty eventually retreated across the bridge but was pursued too closely to destroy it. When Johnson pushed quickly across the damaged span, Minty withdrew. Resuming his advance, Johnson soon

Reed's Bridge was an important crossing point of Chickamauga Creek. A.R. Waud's illustration shows Forrest's Cavalry driving Minty's Union Cavalry from the site on September 18, 1863.

(LC)

reached William Jay's steam sawmill. There the Jay's Mill Road continued south to Alexander's Bridge, while the Brotherton Road ran southwest to join the main highway between LaFayette and Chattanooga. Johnson had just started his troops on the Brotherton Road when Major General John Hood joined the column from Catoosa Station. Taking command, Hood ordered Johnson to use the Jay's Mill Road instead and the column resumed its march in the gathering darkness.

Several miles south of Johnson, Walker's Reserve Corps attempted to force its own crossing of the Chickamauga. Alexander's Bridge was defended by elements of Wilder's mounted infantry brigade. Unlike Minty, Wilder placed his primary line of defense west of the creek. The firepower of his repeating rifles gave him confidence that he could hold his position against great odds. Unaware of his technological inferiority, Walker attacked Wilder with a brigade of Brigadier General St. John Liddell's division. Although the unit suffered 105 casualties, it could make no progress. Having learned a hard lesson, Walker left Wilder's front and headed northward to Byram's Ford, an unguarded crossing a mile downstream. There, far behind schedule, he finally got his units across the creek and turned south in accordance with Bragg's plan. Learning that Minty's loss of Reed's Bridge had compromised his left flank, Wilder meanwhile withdrew to the southwest and established a new blocking position east of the LaFayette Road.

As darkness fell on September 18, Bragg's offensive was seriously behind its projected timetable. Johnson's division had marched southward on the Viniard-Alexander Road until it halted in front of Wilder's blockade. Walker had finally gotten his two small divisions west of the creek, but his troops were scattered for a mile along the road behind Johnson. Buckner had managed to push only one brigade across the creek at Thedford's Ford. Polk was still facing Crittenden at Lee and Gordon's Mill, while Hill's corps guarded crossing sites even further south. Nevertheless, Bragg believed he had successfully turned the Federal flank and next day would be able

General John Bell Hood

(LC)

A COMMON MISCONCEPTION OF THE BATTLE OF CHICKAMAUGA WAS THAT IT WAS FOUGHT ALONG THE BANKS OF CHICKAMAUGA CREEK. THIS KURZ AND ALLISON LITHOGRAPH, CREATED BY ARTISTS NOT PRESENT AT THE BATTLE, HELPED REINFORCE THIS IMPRESSION.

(LC)

to descend upon Crittenden in a massive coordinated attack. Unknown to Bragg, Rosecrans during the afternoon unwittingly invalidated that assumption by ordering Thomas to pass behind Crittenden and march northward throughout the night. Rosecrans's decision placed the Federal army's left flank far north of where Bragg expected to find it when the battle opened on the next day.

Early on September 19, thirsty Federal soldiers from Colonel Daniel McCook's brigade of Granger's Reserve Corps pushed beyond their picket line in search of water near Jay's Mill. McCook's men had moved from their camp near Rossville, Georgia, on the previous day in response to Minty's call for assistance. Arriving near Jay's Mill long after Minty had departed, McCook had captured several prisoners who indicated their unit had recently crossed Reed's Bridge. Unwilling to approach the bridge at night, McCook established a defensive position several hundred yards northwest of Jay's Mill and waited for daylight. A similar distance south of the mill, pickets from the First Georgia Cavalry also waited for morning. Under orders to screen Hood's right and rear, Brigadier General Henry Davidson of Forrest's Cavalry Corps had encountered McCook's pickets and recoiled in the darkness. At dawn Davidson sent the First Georgia forward again and they soon struck some of McCook's men at a small spring near the mill. McCook meanwhile had sent a regiment to destroy Reed's Bridge, but again it was only damaged.

Ordered back to Rossville by Granger, McCook withdrew with Davidson's cavalrymen in pursuit. At the LaFayette Road he found Thomas, whose leading elements had just arrived after an all-night march from Crawfish Springs.

ROSECRANS'S HEADQUARTERS ON SEPTEMBER 17 AND 18, 1863, WAS THIS HOUSE AT CRAWFISH SPRINGS. IT ALSO SERVED AS A UNION HOSPITAL.

(*BL*)

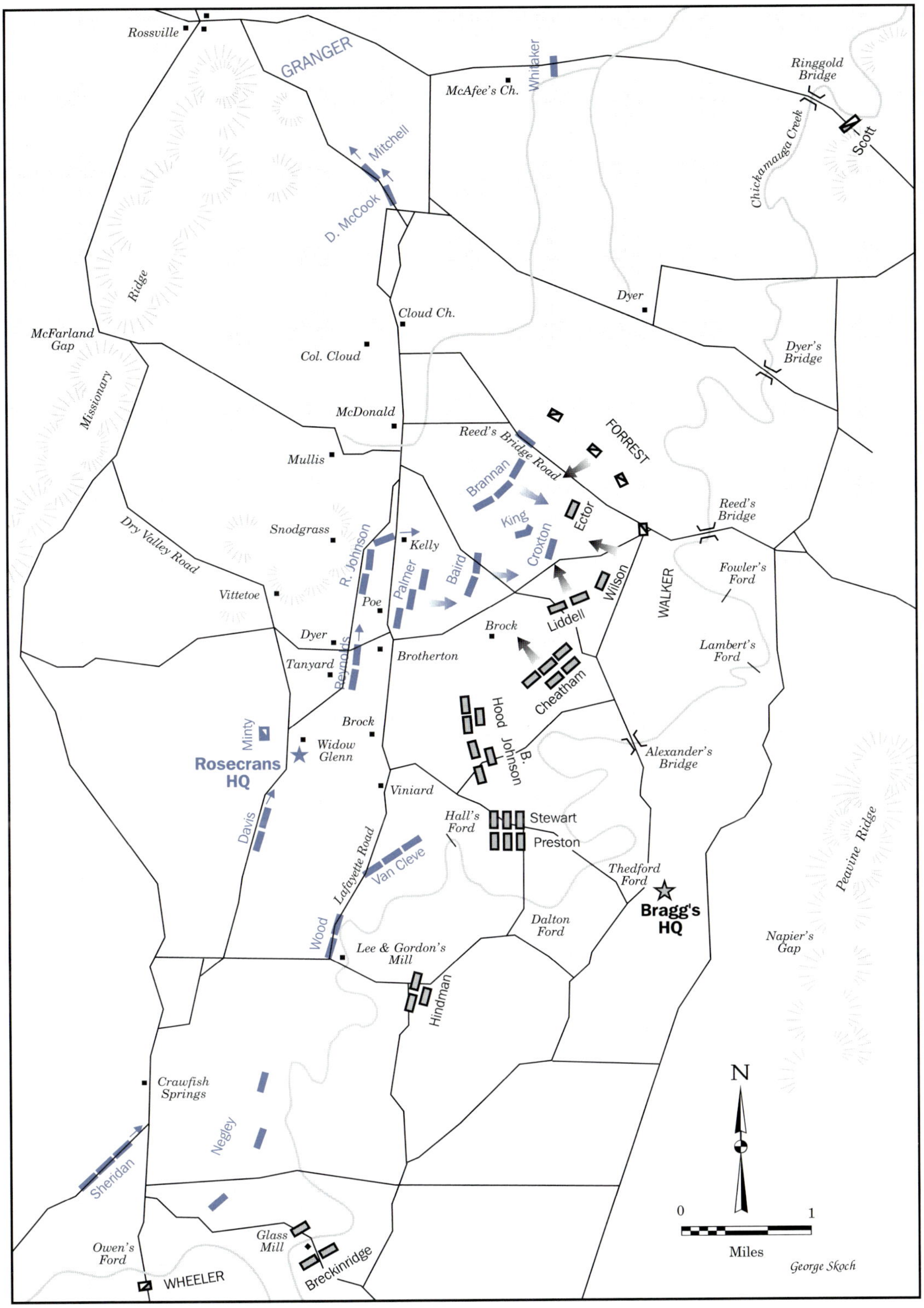

7 A.M. TO NOON, SATURDAY, SEPTEMBER 19, 1863

Believing he could capture an isolated Confederate infantry brigade near Jay's Mill, Thomas sent Brannan's division eastward from the Kelly Farm. Instead, Brannan surprised Forrest's cavalry. Forrest was soon reinforced by Walker's infantry division. Baird's division relieved Brannan's, only to be driven off by Liddell.

These movements indicated the general pattern of the fighting on September 19. The battle would flow from north to south as each side fed one division at a time into the fight. Most divisions marched from the south to the north before turning toward their enemy. By accident or design, many units would strike their adversary's southern flank, or in turn be struck in their own southern flank.

McCook reported that a single Confederate infantry brigade had crossed Chickamauga Creek and was trapped on the west side. In response, Thomas ordered Brigadier General John Brannan's division to destroy the Confederate unit. Brannan deployed Colonel Ferdinand Van Derveer's brigade on the Reed's Bridge Road and Colonel John Croxton's brigade on a woods path on Van Derveer's right. Colonel John Connell's brigade followed the leading brigades as a reserve. Around 7:30 A.M. Davidson's men encountered Croxton's skirmishers and sent them fleeing to their main body. In turn, the horsemen recoiled from Croxton's advancing regiments. Seeing the panic-stricken cavalrymen dashing from the woods, Forrest formed Davidson's dismounted troopers in a defensive line just west of Jay's Field. Croxton brought his five regiments up to face Davidson and the battle was on.

Unable to determine Forrest's strength, Croxton cautiously engaged the Confederates but did not resume his advance. Riding in search of reinforcements, Forrest found Bragg and Walker near Alexander's Bridge and requested the loan of an infantry unit. Walker provided Colonel Claudius Wilson's brigade, which moved north around 9:00 A.M. Hitting Croxton's flank, Wilson forced the Federal commander to change front to protect his right. About the same time that Wilson went into action, Forrest deployed Colonel George Dibrell's brigade to protect his own right flank. Advancing dismounted in the vicinity of the Reed's Bridge Road, Dibrell's men encountered Van Derveer's brigade and were halted by its fire. To meet this new threat, Forrest commandeered Brigadier General Matthew Ector's brigade of the Reserve Corps without Walker's knowledge. Ector replaced Dibrell, but he too was unable to drive Van Derveer from his position. Forrest had stabilized the Confederate line, but he could not gain ground against Brannan's division.

When Brannan's troops began to exhaust their ammunition, Thomas sent Brigadier General Absalom Baird's division to their assistance. Like Brannan before him, Baird advanced westward through the woods with two brigades in his front line and one in reserve. Coming upon Croxton's weary men, Brigadier General John King's brigade relieved them and continued the battle against their mostly unseen opponents. Unique in the Army of the Cumberland, King's brigade consisted entirely of regular army units. Extending King's line southward was Colonel Benjamin Scribner's brigade, while Colonel John Starkweather's brigade remained in reserve. North of Baird, Van Derveer's brigade and part of Connell's brigade maintained their original position on the

THIS ROMANTICIZED PAINTING BY THOMAS NAST DEPICTS THE MOMENT WHEN LIEUTENANT GEORGE W. VAN PELT'S BATTERY A, FIRST MICHIGAN LIGHT ARTILLERY, WAS OVERRUN BY THE CONFEDERATE DIVISION OF ST. JOHN R. LIDDELL.

(COURTESY OF CHICAGO HISTORICAL SOCIETY)

road. Like Forrest, Thomas had now stabilized his battle line; unlike Forrest, whose forces were small and weakly armed, Thomas had enough combat power in Brannan's and Baird's divisions to drive the Confederates. Accordingly, Scribner and King gained ground against Wilson and Ector.

Nearer the action than Rosecrans, who was just leaving Crawfish Springs, Bragg could influence the situation more quickly than his opponent. Thus when he committed Liddell's division to the fight, Thomas had no fresh force immediately available to counter it. Forming Colonel Daniel Govan's and Brigadier General Edward Walthall's brigades along the Alexander's Bridge Road, Liddell sent them toward Baird's right flank. First to be hit was Scribner's brigade on the west edge of the Winfrey Field. Facing in two directions when Liddell's men came screaming down upon them, Scribner's regiments disintegrated. Liddell next encountered Starkweather's brigade, which also broke for the rear in panic. Baird's last hope was King's brigade, but King too was caught changing formation and the regulars fled north through Van Derveer's brigade. Van Derveer waited grimly for Liddell's men to appear through the underbrush, then unleashed a tremendous volley in their faces. Winded after their long advance, Liddell's brigades sullenly withdrew. Their departure was hastened by the return of Croxton's brigade, which pushed Liddell's exhausted troops eastward beyond the Winfrey Field.

The respite gained by Liddell's repulse was fleeting, as Bragg now threw another division into the fight. Major General Benjamin Cheatham's five-brigade division was the largest in the Army of Tennessee. Part of Polk's corps, Cheatham around 7:00 A.M. had crossed to the west bank of the Chickamauga at Dalton's Ford. Ordered northward by Bragg around 11:00 A.M., the division was now available to extend the Confederate line. As Liddell's division halted its withdrawal, Cheatham's men began to form on its left. Cheatham placed three brigades in his front line, from left to right the units of Brigadier

HAND-TO-HAND COMBAT AT THE BATTLE LINES IS CAPTURED IN THIS PAINTING BY WILLIAM TRAVIS.

(COURTESY OF SMITHSONIAN INSTITUTION)

Generals Marcus Wright, Preston Smith, and John Jackson. In the division's second line were the brigades of Brigadier Generals Otho Strahl and George Maney. As soon as his command was formed in line of battle, Cheatham advanced. He soon encountered Croxton's brigade and, far overlapping its line, easily began to push it westward. By 12:30 P.M. Cheatham had gained the crest of a slight ridge 400 yards west of the intersection of the Alexander's Bridge and Brotherton roads.

No sooner was Croxton's brigade out of Cheatham's sight than it was replaced

THE CREATION OF THE FIRST NATIONAL MILITARY PARK

"Be it enacted by the Senate and House of Representatives of the United States of America in Congress assembled, That for the purposes of preserving and suitably marking for historical and professional military study the fields of some of the most remarkable maneuvers and most brilliant fighting in the war of the rebellion." Thus begins the legislation that established Chickamauga and Chattanooga National Military Park as the first so designated park on August 19, 1890.

The idea of establishing a National Military Park began with General Ferdinand Van Derveer, an officer of the Army of Cumberland, on his second visit to the battlefield, the first being on two bloody days in September 1863. He was a Washington newspaper correspondent for the *Cincinnati Commercial Gazette* when he returned to Chickamauga in June 1888. It was during a series of letters to the newspaper that the idea to preserve Chickamauga Battlefield began to take form. "The survivors of the Army of the Cumberland should awake to great pride in this notable field of Chickamauga. Why should it not, as well as eastern fields, be marked by monuments, and its lines be accurately preserved for history? There was no more magnificent fighting during the war than both armies did there. Both sides might well unite in preserving the field where both, in a military sense, won such renown."

Whereas Gettysburg at the time had only the Union side represented, it was proposed that Chickamauga have both Union and Confederate positions marking the field, making it most unique and at the same time providing a healing process.

When the Society of the Army of the Cumberland met a few weeks later, a committee was formed whose purpose was to initiate a movement for the purchase of the ground where the Battle of Chickamauga was fought. It was recommended that monuments be placed to mark the location of the troops that fought there and that it be preserved similar to Gettysburg.

At the first meeting of the newly formed committee in Washington on February 13, 1889, it was agreed to invite the Confederate veterans of the battle of Chickamauga who were in Washington at the time. The united committee became known as the Joint Chickamauga Memorial Association.

The objectives of the association were declared in the charter to be "to mark and preserve the battle field of Chickamauga, on which were fought the actions of September eighteenth, nineteenth, and twentieth, Anno Domini, one thousand eight hundred and sixty-three, together with the natural and artificial features, as they were at the time of said battle, by such memorial stones, tablets, or monuments as a generous people may aid to erect, to commemorate the valor displayed by American soldiers on that field."

On September 19, 1889, a joint meeting of Union and Confederate veterans was called to be held in Chattanooga to consider the subject of the Chickamauga Park. Many notable veterans of the Battle of Chickamauga gave

The Wilder Brigade Monument was erected at the site of the Widow Glenn's house, which was Rosecrans's headquarters on September 19, 1863.

(NPS)

addresses that day, exactly 26 years after the battle, among them Union General William Rosecrans. Rosecrans's speech best instills the feelings of the veterans at that time. He begins: "This occasion is one for which you will look through history in vain to find a second. To-day twenty-six years ago began the great bloody battle of Saturday, the 19th day of September, 1863, within twelve miles of this place, and the survivors of that battle, both Blue and Gray, and the people who to-day enjoy the fruits which grew out of that battle, are assembled together to consider how they shall make it a national memorial ground, which people of all time shall come and visit with the interest due to the greatness of the events which occurred on that battle ground. One of the most noble features to me of this occasion is this: It is very difficult to find in history an instance where contending parties in after years meet together in perfect amity. It took great men to win that battle, but it takes greater men still, I will say morally greater, to wipe away all the ill feeling which naturally grows out of such a contest." Following Rosecrans's address General Henry Van Ness Boynton (a Union colonel at Chickamauga), spoke of making Chickamauga a "western Gettysburg, [but] the lines of both armies should be equally marked."

On September 20, 1889 a huge barbecue was held in Crawfish Springs, Georgia (present day Chickamauga). The barbecue was attended by 12,000 people, making it one of the largest barbecues held in the South. This festive occasion culminated the charter to establish Chickamauga battlefield as a park. Representatives from each state which had troops at Chickamauga were chosen as incorporators.

Some of the land was acquired through the aid of Congress. Additional acreage was requested on Lookout Mountain and Missionary Ridge to commemorate the Battle of Chattanooga. Collectively, the acquired land was to be preserved as Chickamauga and Chattanooga National Military Park.

The bill to establish Chickamauga and Chattanooga National Military Park passed through the House in twenty-three minutes. In the Senate the bill moved even faster, a mere twenty minutes. That same night the bill was taken to President Benjamin Harrison and signed. The bill provided for fifteen square miles.

On September 19 and 20, 1895, Chickamauga and Chattanooga National Military Park was formally dedicated. It was the nation's first national military park and set a precedent for subsequent national military parks. As stated in the enabling legislation, the battlefield was used for military study and the War Department was in charge until 1933. In 1933 the reigns of jurisdiction were passed over to the National Park Service, which has been the caretaker ever since.

The Second Minnesota Monument on Snodgrass Hill is one of four monuments erected to this regiment in Chickamauga and Chattanooga National Military Park.

(NPS)

The monuments along postwar Battleline Road mark Union positions on September 20, 1863.

(NPS)

The attack of Stewart's Confederate division on September 19, 1863, relieved the pressure on the left flank of Benjamin Franklin Cheatham.

(USAMHI)

by Brigadier General Richard Johnson's division of McCook's corps. Johnson had begun the day in McLemore's Cove but had been ordered forward in haste by Rosecrans. Placed under Thomas's command, Johnson was told to form a line of battle and advance eastward. Moving in the traditional formation of two brigades forward and one in reserve, Johnson arrived just as Cheatham chased Croxton's men toward the LaFayette Road. Johnson's front line, Colonel Philemon Baldwin's and Brigadier General August Willich's brigades, struck Jackson's Brigade and halted its pursuit of Croxton. For a time Jackson held his own against the more numerous Federals, but with his ammunition running low and casualties depleting his ranks, he called for aid. Cheatham replaced Jackson with Brigadier General George Maney's small brigade. Maney's men were no match for two Federal brigades, and when both of his flanks collapsed he hastily withdrew.

A postwar photo of General Alexander Peter Stewart, who would become one of the first commissioners of the Chickamauga Battlefield Park.

(NPS)

Meanwhile, Johnson's division regained the Winfrey Field and some woods to the south.

Shortly after Johnson arrived, several more Federal units reached the field. At Lee and Gordon's Mill Major General John Palmer's division received orders around 11:00 A.M. to assist the Fourteenth Corps. On reaching the battlefield, Palmer placed the brigades of Brigadier General William Hazen, Brigadier General Charles Cruft, and Colonel William Grose in a single line. Crashing southeastward into the forest, the division soon encountered Smith's and Wright's Confederates. Taking the brunt of Palmer's attack in the Brock Field, Smith called for relief and was replaced by Strahl's brigade. No better able to stand the Federal fire than Smith, Strahl's men soon withdrew also. Following Palmer's division up the LaFayette Road were two brigades of Brigadier General Horatio Van Cleve's division of the Twenty-first Corps. They soon appeared on the left flank of Wright's brigade. Brigadier General Samuel Beatty's brigade soon wrecked Wright's command and it joined Cheatham's other units in retreat. South of Beatty, Colonel George Dick's brigade extended the Federal line. Beyond Dick, Colonel Edward King's brigade of Major General Joseph Reynolds's

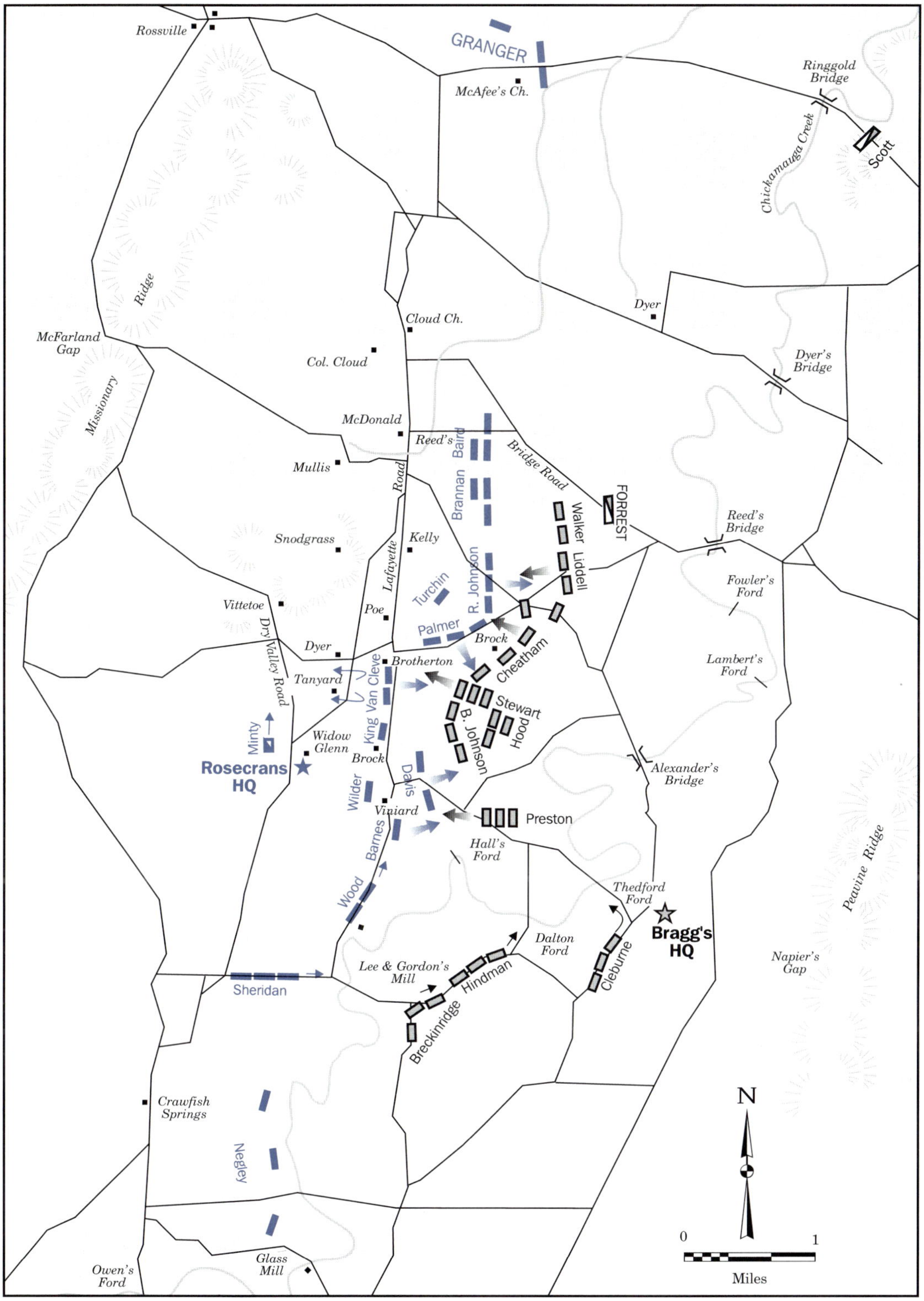

NOON TO MID-AFTERNOON, SATURDAY, SEPTEMBER 19, 1863

The strength of Cheatham's Confederate division's attack necessitated several reinforcements to Richard Johnson's and Palmer's Union divisions. The help of Reynolds and Van Cleve's Federals finally caused Cheatham's withdrawal.

On Cheatham's left, Stewart's division attacked in column and drove back elements of Palmer, Van Cleve, and Reynolds. Stewart's momentum carried him across the Lafayette Road near the Brotherton Farm, penetrating the developing Federal line. Farther to the south, Jefferson C. Davis's Federal division encountered Confederates east of the Chattanooga-Lafayette Road.

As a result of the southward flow of the fighting, units that had fought in the opening actions had disengaged and were resting and reorganizing.

division also faced eastward in the woods. In the field south of George Brotherton's modest cabin Reynolds gathered several batteries as a reserve.

The defeat of Cheatham's division by Johnson, Palmer, and Van Cleve did not prove decisive, and again it was Bragg's turn to alter the balance. Since early morning Major General Alexander Stewart's division had been waiting patiently near Thedford's Ford. Around noon Bragg ordered Stewart to report to Polk and enter the battle. Stewart marched north through the forest to the Brock Farm, where he encountered Wright's retreating brigade. Apprised of Van Cleve's position on his left, Stewart resolved to strike that unit on his own authority. Forming his division

The Brotherton Farmstead was the scene of Confederate penetrations on both September 19 and 20, 1863. This photograph was taken circa 1898.

(NPS)

into a column of brigades, he turned west with Brigadier General Henry Clayton's brigade in the lead. Confronting Beatty's, Dick's, and Grose's Federals, Clayton's troops stood their ground and fired until their ammunition was expended. Stewart then replaced Clayton's men with Brigadier General John Brown's brigade. With a yell Brown's regiments drove Beatty's and Dick's troops from the woods east of the LaFayette Road. There Brown paused, his energy momentarily spent.

Sensing that the Federals who had withdrawn behind Reynolds's guns in the Brotherton Field were shaky, Stewart committed his last brigade, Brigadier General William Bate's. Bate burst from the forest shortly after 3:30 P.M. and quickly routed Van Cleve's division. Hazen's brigade, which was nearby replenishing ammunition, attempted to assist Van Cleve but was also swept westward. At approximately the same time, Colonel James Sheffield's brigade from Hood's division entered the fight on Bate's right and drove back Grose's and Cruft's brigades. A counterattack by Brigadier General John Turchin's brigade of Reynolds's division halted Sheffield, but for a time nothing could stop Bate's rampaging Confederates. With Van Cleve's soldiers fleeing madly before him, Bate raced through the Brotherton Field and finally into the south end of the Dyer Field. There Stewart and Bate paused to survey their surroundings. They had created a major rupture in the Federal line, but without reinforcement they could not remain in their advanced position. Seeing Federal troops approaching from both flanks, Stewart sadly ordered Bate to withdraw east of the LaFayette Road.

During his march north Stewart had passed behind Bushrod Johnson's division of Hood's corps. This division remained undisturbed until shortly after 2:00 P.M. when it was approached by Brigadier General Jefferson Davis's two-brigade division of the Twentieth Corps. Ordered north by Rosecrans from Crawfish Spring, Davis quickly found himself in trouble. On Davis's left Colonel Hans Heg's brigade was counterattacked by Johnson, who forced it across the LaFayette Road. Having vanquished the immediate Federal threat, Hood ordered the Confederate advance to continue. Johnson crossed the LaFayette

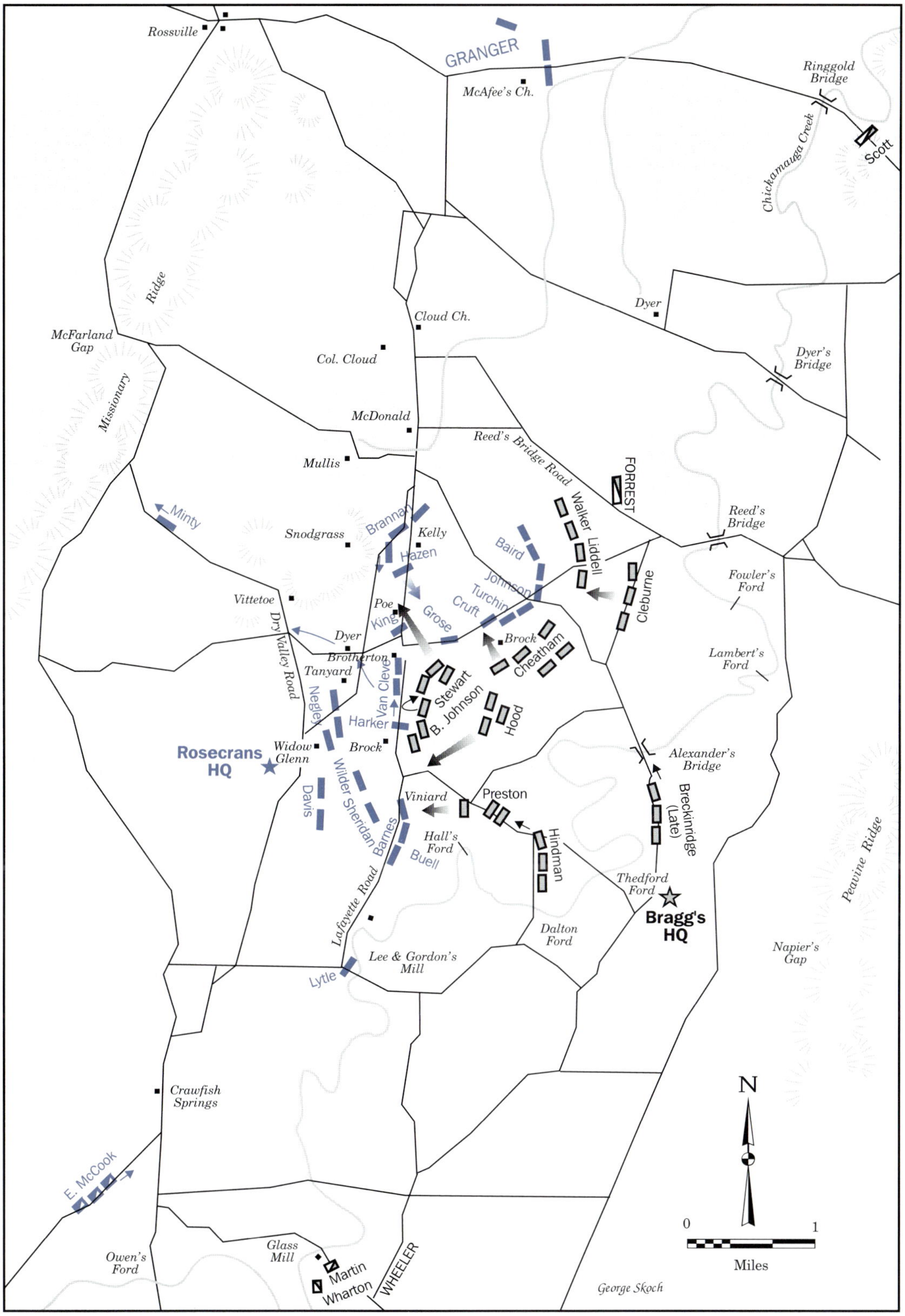

MID-AFTERNOON TO DARK, SATURDAY, SEPTEMBER 19, 1863

Stewart's penetration across Lafayette Road was a crisis for the Federals. Stewart had attacked without support. As a result, Palmer's, Reynolds's, and Van Cleve's divisions were able to stop Stewart. The arrival of Negley's division, and the movement of Brannan's, forced Stewart back to the east side of the road.

Bushrod Johnson's division attacked to the south of Stewart, but was in turn driven back by Federals. In the area of the Viniard Farm, Davis's division, aided by Wood's, fought elements of Confederate divisions under Bushrod Johnson and Hood. Hood's attack drove Davis and Wood back, but Wilder's brigade, fighting on foot from a well-chosen position, stopped Hood's attack. The arrival of Sheridan's division stabilized the situation for the Federals.

At the northern part of the field, Cleburne's fresh division, supported by Cheatham's, attacked at dark striking Thomas's troops. This confusing fight was inconclusive, and Thomas pulled back that night to better defensive positions.

Road with two brigades abreast and one in reserve, but his neat formations soon unraveled. On his right Colonel John Fulton's brigade drifted to the northwest, where it routed King's brigade and inadvertently assisted Bate in clearing the Brotherton Field. On Johnson's left Brigadier General John Gregg's regiments were checked by Wilder's brigade, which now occupied a reserve position at the western edge of the Viniard Farm. When Gregg was seriously wounded, his brigade advanced no further. Called forward by Johnson, Brigadier General Evander McNair's brigade also fragmented, with two regiments briefly crossing the

THESE MONUMENTS REPRESENT UNION TROOPS ENGAGED AT THE VINIARD FARM AGAINST SOLDIERS OF THE CONFEDERATE LEFT FLANK, SEPTEMBER 19, 1863.

(NPS)

LaFayette Road and the remainder following Fulton to the northwest.

As Johnson's attack stalled, Brigadier General Thomas Wood's two-brigade division reached the field. Ordered northward around 3:00 P.M. from Lee and Gordon's Mill, Wood posted Colonel George Buell's brigade north of the Viniard House, then continued up the LaFayette Road with Colonel Charles Harker's brigade. Arriving in the rear of Fulton's and McNair's regiments, Harker fired into the backs of the surprised Confederates. The unexpected fire stunned Johnson's men, and they fled to safety in the woods east of the road. Aware that he was isolated, Harker quickly withdrew to the west. South of Harker, Buell's men had hardly taken position when they were assaulted by part of Brigadier General Evander Law's division. Passing behind Johnson's command, the brigades of Brigadier Generals Jerome Robertson and Henry Benning pushed southwest toward the Viniard Field. Brushing aside Brigadier General William Carlin's brigade of Davis's division, they violently struck Buell and sent him flying behind Wilder's line. Rushing forward, Robertson's and Benning's men reached a drainage ditch in front of Wilder's position but could advance no further.

MAJOR GENERAL PATRICK RONAYNE CLEBURNE

(BL)

Several times before sunset Crittenden, Wood, and Davis mounted unsuccessful counterattacks to regain the ground around the Viniard House. In one of these futile advances brigade commander Hans Heg was mortally wounded leading his men toward the LaFayette Road. Finally, late in the day Rosecrans threw into the fight at Viniard's virtually his last reserve. When Wood's division had left Lee and Gordon's Mill, its place had been taken by Sheridan's division of McCook's corps. Now Sheridan was needed at Viniard's to strengthen the efforts to regain the LaFayette Road. Leaving one brigade at the mill, Sheridan marched north with the brigades of Colonels Luther Bradley and Bernard Laiboldt. Bradley's brigade entered the fight first and, although its commander was wounded, it carried the day. Heavily outnumbered, Robertson's and Benning's men finally relinquished their hold on the Viniard Field and withdrew eastward into the forest. Behind them the field was carpeted with the dead and wounded of both sides, silent testimony to the intensity of the struggle for its possession.

As night approached, the sounds of conflict were gradually dying away when, suddenly, on the north end of the battlefield the roar of gunfire broke out anew. Trying to preserve his original concept of driving the Federals southward, Bragg in mid-afternoon had ordered Daniel H. Hill to send Major General Patrick Cleburne's division to join Polk's effort on the army's right. By 6:00 P.M. Cleburne was in position behind Walker's corps facing the Winfrey

Field. That sector had been quiet for several hours as the fighting had migrated to the south. Nor did the Federal units west of the Winfrey Field desire to upset the equilibrium. Thomas had chosen a better defensive position nearer the LaFayette Road, and he had begun to withdraw his divisions to the new line. Momentarily left behind was Richard Johnson's division, which would cover the withdrawal of Thomas's other units. Ready to assist Johnson was Baird's division, now reconstituted after its morning rout.

At sunset Cleburne's division swept forward with all three brigades abreast. On Cleburne's right Brigadier General Lucius Polk's brigade overlapped Colonel Philemon Baldwin's position. In the center Brigadier General Sterling Wood's brigade crossed the Winfrey Field to hit Baldwin frontally. On the left Brigadier General James Deshler's brigade headed through the woods toward the brigades of Brigadier General August Willich and Colonel Joseph Dodge. Amid the smoke from burning underbrush and the gathering darkness, Cleburne's assault soon degenerated into chaos. Advancing to support Baldwin, some of Baird's men mistakenly fired into their friends, who returned the fire. Attempting to lead a counterattack, Baldwin was killed. On the Confederate side part of Wood's brigade disintegrated, while Deshler's brigade missed the Federal line entirely. As Brigadier General Preston Smith led his brigade forward to support Deshler, he mistakenly rode into Federal lines and was shot down by Dodge's brigade. Smith's killers then found themselves surrounded. By 9:00 P.M., when the confusing melee ended, Johnson and Baird had been driven back to Thomas's new line, leaving the Winfrey Field to Cleburne's exhausted men.

ILLUSTRATION FROM *HARPER'S WEEKLY* SHOWS THOMAS'S MEN REPULSING THE CHARGE OF THE CONFEDERATES.

The Winfrey Field fight was sputtering to a close when the leaders of the Army of the Cumberland gathered in the modest cabin of widow Eliza Glenn on the south edge of the battlefield. The discussion quickly focused upon courses of action for the next day. The choices were: attack, retreat, or stand firmly on the

THIS PAINTING BY THOMAS BUCHANAN REID DEPICTS THE MAIN HOUSE OF THE KELLY FARMSTEAD THAT BURNED THE AFTERNOON OF SEPTEMBER 20, 1863.

(NPS)

defensive. With only five relatively fresh brigades, the army had been too badly hurt to go on the offensive. Retreat was also out of the question, especially with Assistant Secretary of War Charles Dana present. If the army held its ground on the next day, Bragg might retreat, as he had done after Perryville and Stones River. Thus Rosecrans concluded that the Army of the Cumberland must stand. Thomas would maintain his present position, a roughly north-south line with a salient bending east of the LaFayette Road to encompass the Kelly Farm. On Thomas's right, McCook would withdraw from the Viniard Field and anchor his right near the Widow Glenn's. Crittenden would place his two weakened divisions in reserve behind the army's right center. Granger, who had reached Rossville with part of the Reserve Corps, was telegraphed to be prepared to support Thomas if necessary.

Little more than two miles away at Thedford's Ford, Bragg met individually with his commanders. Unhappy with the disjointed way in which the battle had been fought and perhaps distrustful of Hill and Buckner, Bragg had decided to divide his army into two wings. First to arrive was Leonidas Polk. Although he harbored grave reservations about Polk's competence, Bragg felt compelled to give his most senior subordinate a wing commander's role. Polk's right wing consisted of Hill's corps, Walker's corps, and Cheatham's division. With those forces Polk would initiate the army's assault on the Federal left at daybreak. Beginning with Polk's rightmost division, the attack would roll southward sequentially and drive the Federals away from Chattanooga. Aware that James Longstreet had reached the area, Bragg assigned him the left wing, composed of Hood's corps, Buckner's corps, and Hindman's division of Polk's corps. When Longstreet finally appeared around 11:00 P.M., he too received his instructions, then lay down in the woods to rest. Only the army's third lieutenant general, Harvey Hill, was unapprised of the plan, although he learned from a staff officer that he had been subordinated to Polk.

Upon leaving Bragg, Polk rode to his own headquarters near Alexander's Bridge. He was accompanied by Major General John Breckinridge, one of Hill's division commanders. While Polk and Breckinridge chatted, Polk's staff prepared written orders for Hill, Walker, and Cheatham and dispatched them by courier. Walker and Cheatham received their assignments, but the courier seeking Hill could not find him. Returning to headquarters, the courier was not permitted to disturb anyone, so he returned to his unit without transmitting the vital information that Hill had not received his orders. Similarly, Breckinridge apparently left Polk's camp with no inkling that a dawn attack was contemplated and that his division was to initiate it. As for Hill himself, when he reached Alexander's Bridge around 4:00 A.M. the guards that had been posted to guide him had retired for the evening. Disgusted, Hill turned and rode to join his corps near the Winfrey Field. He was still unaware of his role in the coming day's fight.

During the night of September 19 a weather front passed over the battlefield, causing the temperature to plummet and increasing the suffering of the thousands of wounded lying in the woods. In the valley of Chickamauga Creek dense fog developed. Elsewhere, the smoke from the previous day's battle hung heavily in the air. Awakening around 5:00 A.M., Polk soon discovered that no orders had reached Hill. In haste, Polk's staff drafted new orders to Breckinridge and Cleburne and sent them off shortly after 5:30 A.M. Thirty minutes later, a courier found Hill in company with his two subordinates just west of the Winfrey Field. In a written response to Polk, later amplified verbally to Bragg, Hill complained that several things would have to be done before his corps could attack. His line overlapped adjacent units and would have to be adjusted; the enemy line had not been reconnoitered and would have to be scouted; and his own troops had not finished receiving their breakfast rations. Disgruntled, Bragg acquiesced in the delay.

While the Confederates dawdled, Rosecrans rode to the north end of his line. There he found the intersection of the Lafayette and McFarland's Gap roads unprotected. To cover the junction, Thomas requested Major General James Negley's division, a Fourteenth Corps unit in McCook's sector. Rosecrans approved the request, specifying that McCook was to replace Negley. Riding southward a little later, Rosecrans discovered that Negley had not been relieved. Ordering Negley to send his reserve brigade to Thomas at once, Rosecrans told Crittenden to fill Negley's place. After visiting McCook, Rosecrans again rode northward. He found Negley

THE WOODEN BREASTWORKS OF THOMAS'S MEN ARE MISSING FROM THIS DRAWING BY HARRY J. KELLOGG OF THE UNION LINE AT KELLY FIELD.

(NPS)

still in position, with Wood's division just arriving. Impatiently Rosecrans ordered Wood to expedite the relief of Negley's remaining brigades. Camp gossip later asserted that Rosecrans had sulfurously berated Wood in front of his staff, but Wood categorically denied that such an altercation had occurred. Chastised or not, Wood placed Buell's and Harker's brigades,

MORNING TO 11:00 A.M., SUNDAY, SEPTEMBER 20, 1863
During the night the Union army pulled back to defensive positions closer to the Lafayette Road. Thomas, in immediate command of the Union left, requested additional troops to prevent the Confederates from cutting the Union routes to Chattanooga. Rosecrans put Negley's division in motion to the left.

Bragg's plan, as General Thomas anticipated, was to attack the northern section of the Union line and prevent Federal movement to Chattanooga. Polk's wing did not attack until 9:30 A.M. Despite some initial success by Breckinridge, poor coordination and lack of support prevented the Confederates from achieving their objectives. The advance of Breckinridge's division would prompt Federal units to leave their positions farther south in the Union line, to reinforce the threatened northern end.

Cleburne's division attacked alone against Union breastworks on a mile-wide front. Only Stewart's Division of Longstreet's wing was engaged by 11:00 A.M.

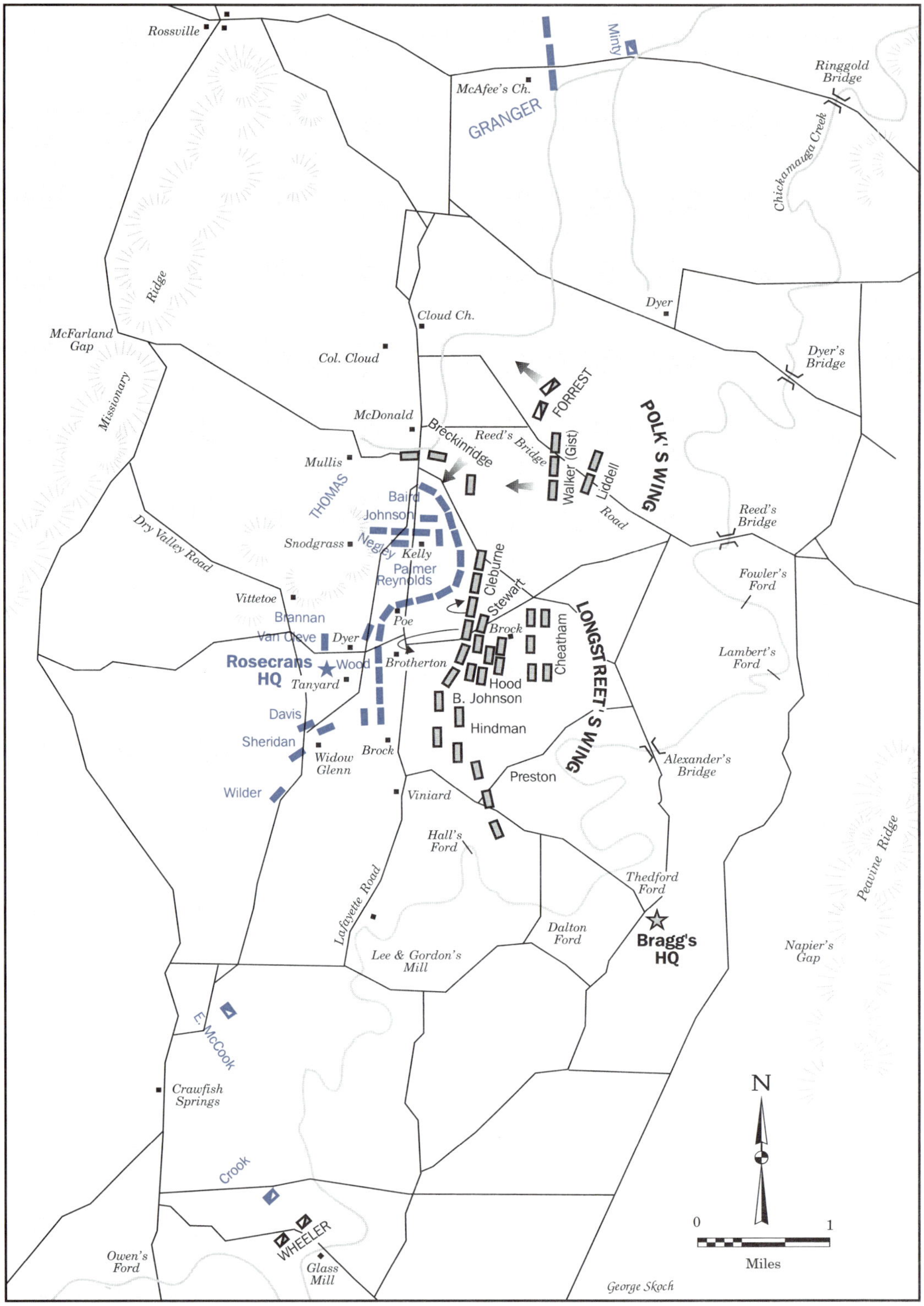

plus Colonel Sidney Barnes's brigade from Van Cleve's division, into Negley's position.

At 9:30 A.M., as Negley headed north, Breckinridge's division began the movement that signaled the beginning of Bragg's attack. Breckinridge advanced with the brigades of Brigadier Generals Benjamin Helm, Marcellus Stovall, and Daniel Adams arrayed in one long line. On the left, Helm's Kentucky Brigade soon encountered the Federal position at the point where it began to bend back to the west. Thomas's men had worked all night felling trees to create a makeshift breastwork, and the effort now paid dividends. Some of the Kentuckians halted, and when Helm tried to energize them he was mortally wounded. Helm's loss rendered his

CONFEDERATE BRIGADIER GENERAL BENJAMIN HARDIN HELM WAS MORTALLY WOUNDED WHILE LEADING HIS BRIGADE OF KENTUCKIANS AT CHICKAMAUGA.

(*TRIUMPH AT CHICKAMAUGA* BY JOHN PAUL STRAIN. PHOTO COURTESY OF NEWMARK PUBLISHING, LOUISVILLE, KENTUCKY)

brigade ineffective for the remainder of the day. On Helm's right, however, Stovall and Adams pressed ahead against light resistance. Approaching the Rossville–McFarland's Gap Road intersection, Stovall and Adams shattered Brigadier General John Beatty's brigade of Negley's division, spread thinly across a division-sized sector. Realizing he was beyond the Federal flank, Breckinridge turned southward and began to advance along both sides of the LaFayette Road.

Brushing aside Beatty's fleeing remnants, Stovall and Adams charged toward the rear of Thomas's Kelly Field perimeter. On their way they swept by the left flank of Colonel Joseph Dodge's brigade, which made no effort to check the Confederate advance. Just as Stovall's men entered the Kelly Field a fresh Federal unit burst from the woods on their right. Colonel Ferdinand Van Derveer's brigade of Brannan's division had been called north from its reserve position as soon as Thomas knew the Confederate attack was serious. Now Van Derveer's men appeared just in front of Stovall's jubilant Confederates. Wheeling to their left, Van Derveer's regiments fired a volley and charged, driving Stovall's soldiers back in confusion. At the same time, Colonel Timothy Stanley's brigade of Negley's division met Adams's brigade west of the LaFayette Road and halted its advance as well. Adams was wounded and left behind as his brigade also withdrew to its starting point. Bragg's plan had finally been executed with two small brigades, but without assistance they were unable to exploit their momentary advantage.

Breckinridge's troops were unsupported because Cleburne's division had been halted by Thomas's barricades. Cleburne had launched his attack soon after Breckinridge but had made no progress against the divisions of Baird, Johnson, Palmer, and Reynolds. In addition, the misalignment of Confederate units had caused two of Cleburne's brigades to become entangled with Stewart's division of the left wing. The confusion was so great that Deshler's brigade was forced to circle to the north before again beginning its advance. When it did assault the Federal works, it made no greater progress than Polk's and Wood's brigades on either side. While checking his men's cartridge boxes, Deshler was disemboweled by a shell. Colonel Roger Mills quickly assumed command, got the men under cover, found some ammunition, and maintained the fire. Nevertheless, no further advance would be made by Cleburne's division. Some distance to the rear, Cheatham's division waited in the woods. It too had been forced from the line by finding left wing troops in its way.

Breckinridge's success and Cleburne's failure opened a wide gap in the middle of Hill's corps. To fill the hole, Hill requested Brigadier General States Rights Gist's brigade, one of Walker's units which had just arrived from Catoosa Station. Gist had been given command of Walker's division, making Colonel Peyton Colquitt the new brigade commander. When called forward, Colquitt advanced without skirmishers because he thought friends were in front. Following much the same route as Helm's brigade an hour earlier, Colquitt's men blundered across the face of Thomas's line. In less than thirty minutes the brigade was wrecked and Colquitt was killed. Walker himself brought the remainder of the division forward to rescue Colquitt's remnants. Unsatisfied, Hill threw Govan's brigade of Liddell's division around the corner of the Federal line in an effort to support Breckinridge. Meeting Stovall's and Adams's men retreating, Govan soon followed them as Federal units counterattacked. By noon, except for Cheatham's idle men, the right wing had fought itself out.

As Rosecrans juggled units, Bragg saw his control of events slipping away. His dawn attack had begun four hours late, and now the sequential advance of divisions had broken down.

Although it failed, Polk's attack sent shock waves down the length of Rosecrans's battle line. Breckinridge's momentary success caused Thomas to dispatch staff officers far and wide for aid. One of those officers, Captain Sanford Kellogg, reached Brannan's division with such a message not long after 10:00 A.M. Brannan was in line west of the Poe Field, sandwiched between Reynolds's division to the north and Wood's division to the south. His reserve brigade was already moving toward Thomas; if his remaining brigades left the line, the flanks of the adjacent units would be exposed.

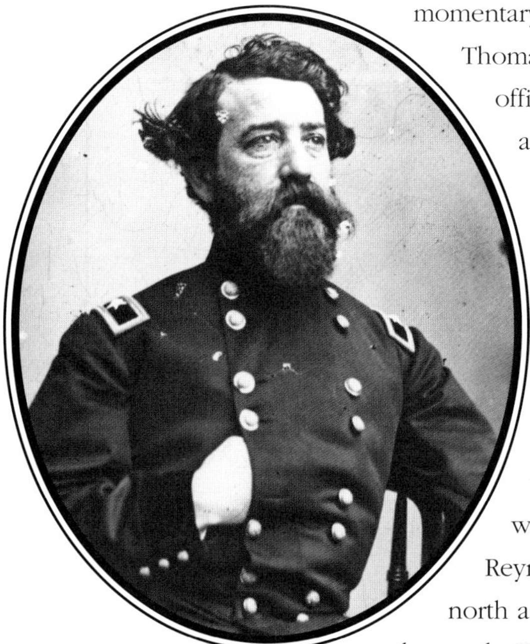

BRIGADIER GENERAL JOHN MILTON BRANNAN (LC)

Rather than create such a hole, Brannan and Kellogg sought Reynolds's counsel. Accepting the necessity for action, Reynolds approved the movement but sent Kellogg to inform Rosecrans of the risks he was assuming. Kellogg found Rosecrans and his staff on a small knoll at the west edge of the Dyer Field. Assuming that Brannan had already left the line, Rosecrans instantly instructed his senior aide-de-camp, Major Frank Bond, to send the following order to Brigadier General Wood: "The general commanding directs that you close up on Reynolds as fast as possible, and support him."

Written at 10:45 A.M., the order was in Wood's hands within five minutes. McCook was present when the order arrived. Aware that Brannan was still on his left, Wood did not understand the context of the order. Further, the order contained two mutually exclusive directives. In the military terminology of the day, to "close up on" another unit usually meant to move adjacent to it, while to "support" meant to get behind it. Because Brannan's presence prevented literal execution of the first directive, Wood's only recourse was to leave the line, march around Brannan, and form behind Reynolds. If Wood moved "as fast as possible," he would leave a gap in the army's battle line that the Confederates could exploit. Could he afford to take such a risk? Because the order was peremptory, could he afford not to? McCook solved Wood's dilemma by arguing that Rosecrans's view of the situation must be superior to theirs and that instant obedience was required. In addition, he offered to replace Wood with Twentieth Corps units. His doubts resolved, Wood ordered his division from the line.

Major General Thomas John Wood

(BL)

As Rosecrans juggled units, Bragg saw his control of events slipping away. His dawn attack had begun four hours late, and now the sequential advance of divisions had broken down. Like Rosecrans, Bragg issued a peremptory order based upon inadequate information. Couriers dashed in all directions carrying Bragg's directive that all commands advance, regardless of the situation. In response, Major General Alexander Stewart, commanding Longstreet's right division, ordered his three brigades forward without reference to the wing commander. Storming westward across the Poe Field, Brown's, Clayton's, and Bate's brigades entered a ring of fire from Brannan's and Reynolds's divisions. Assisted by part of Wood's brigade, some of Stewart's men pushed across the LaFayette Road, momentarily crumbled Brannan's right flank, and stampeded Van Cleve's division in Brannan's rear. When a Federal counterattack erased the gain, the wreckage of Stewart's command receded across the field to its starting point. There would be no breakthrough for Stewart's division this day.

Longstreet also responded to Bragg's peremptory attack order, but at his own pace. While waiting for Polk's attack, he had attempted to place his old corps in the front line, but he had succeeded only in fouling the advance of half of the right wing. Bushrod Johnson's division now stood astride the Brotherton Road, with Stewart's division on its right and Hindman's division on its left. Behind Johnson, whose division was arrayed in two echelons, Law's (formerly Hood's) division waited, also in two echelons. Behind Law, Brigadier General Joseph Kershaw's two-brigade contingent of Major General Lafayette McLaws's division also straddled the road. While Longstreet managed the left wing, Hood handled this three-division column. Held in reserve behind Hindman was Brigadier General William Preston's division of Buckner's corps. Stewart's hasty advance had caught Longstreet by surprise, and he briefly withheld the order to commence the attack. At last, satisfied that all was ready, Longstreet gave the signal and at 11:10 A.M. Johnson's division began to move. It was headed

The 15th U.S. Infantry Regiment helped stop the attacks of Confederate brigades such as Helm's and Peyton H. Colquitt's while behind log breastworks.

(NPS)

11:00 A.M. TO MID-AFTERNOON, SUNDAY, SEPTEMBER 20, 1863

The bulk of Longstreet's wing advances as most of the Federal line at the southern end of the field, is in motion to the north. Davis's and Sheridan's Union divisions are driven from the field. Parts of Negley's and Van Cleve's divisions escort Federal artillery to Chattanooga. Other Federal divisions suffer severely, but their remnants remain on the field.

By noon, Johnson's and Hindman's Confederate divisions have advanced to the Dry Valley Road.

By mid-afternoon, outside of skirmishing, there is little action against the Federal left at the Kelly Farmstead.

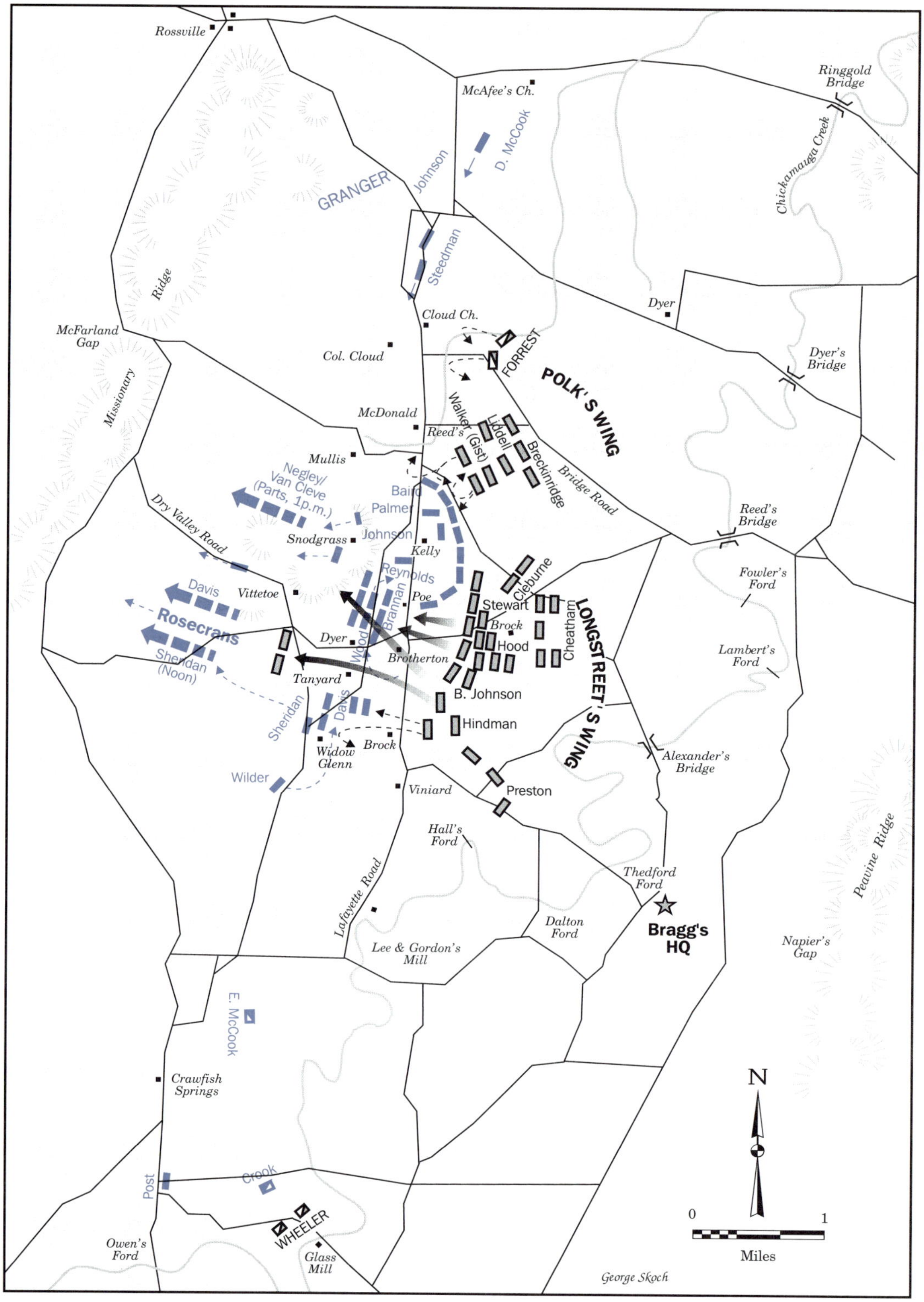

straight for that part of the Federal line being evacuated by Wood's division.

Brushing aside the skirmishers Wood had left behind, Fulton's brigade flowed around the Brotherton House into the gap in the Federal line. On Fulton's right McNair's brigade also made headway, although it met stiff opposition from part of Connell's brigade of Brannan's division.

Entering the woods beyond the Brotherton Field, Johnson's men soon found themselves at the eastern edge of the Dyer Field. In Johnson's words, "the scene now presented was unspeakably grand." Seemingly in panic, Federal troops were running in all directions. At the far side of the field stood several artillery batteries, but they were without infantry support.

Confederate charge against Thomas's line, illustration by A.R. Waud.

(LC)

Still, their frowning presence caused a few moments' hesitation. The spell was broken by the arrival of Colonel Cyrus Sugg's (formerly Gregg's) brigade, which flanked the guns on their right, and by the impetuous advance of Sheffield's brigade, now commanded by Colonel William Perry. Although McNair was wounded, his men joined the grand rush for the guns. Arriving late but willing to share in the credit was Robertson's brigade. Of the twenty-six cannon on the ridge, fifteen fell to the Confederates.

Many of the troops who abandoned the artillerymen belonged to Buell's brigade of Wood's division. Last to leave the line, Buell's regiments had been caught in column and smashed. Wood's remaining brigades did not share Buell's fate. Barnes's brigade reached Thomas's Kelly Field perimeter with little difficulty. Following Barnes was Harker's brigade, which had just left the Dyer Field when Wood halted it.

Seeing the debacle behind him, Wood ordered Harker to counterattack into the field. The brigade's sudden appearance on the flank of the Confederates milling around the captured artillery caused them to break for the rear. McNair's, Perry's, and Robertson's brigades momentarily dissolved into a churning mass as they sought shelter in the woods east of the field. Seeing the rout, Hood ordered Kershaw to deal with Harker, then spurred his horse toward Robertson's Texans, his

Sketch by Frank Vizetelly of the wounding of General Hood.

(Courtesy of the Houghton Library, Harvard University)

old brigade. Just as he reached them, a bullet struck his right thigh and unhorsed him. He was quickly evacuated to a hospital near Alexander's Bridge, where his shattered leg was amputated.

As Kershaw advanced, Wood ordered Harker to make a fighting withdrawal. In the face of increasing pressure, the brigade slowly made its way from the field. Kershaw followed, driving the retreating Federals to the open ridge near the house of George Washington Snodgrass. He then maneuvered his own and Humphreys's brigades into position for an assault on the ridge. He received no assistance from Perry and Robertson, whose brigades gradually recovered their organization during the afternoon but took no further part in the action. Nor would he receive aid from Benning's brigade, which had turned north soon after crossing the LaFayette Road. Driving the two brigades of Brannan's division from the edge of the Poe Field, Benning's men faced northward near the burning Poe House and halted for the afternoon. With Hood incapacitated and Longstreet busy elsewhere, several Confederate brigades dallied while the battle raged with great ferocity just beyond their positions.

With Hood incapacitated and Longstreet busy elsewhere, several Confederate brigades dallied while the battle raged with great ferocity just beyond their positions.

In the southern part of Longstreet's sector, Hindman's division encountered more serious opposition than Hood. On the right Brigadier General Zachariah Deas's brigade drove back both Carlin's and Heg's (now Colonel John Martin's) brigades of Davis's division. Entering the south end of the Dyer Field, Deas's exultant troops also shattered Colonel Bernard Laiboldt's brigade of Sheridan's division. Hastily thrown into action by McCook while still in column, Laiboldt's regiments had no chance to defend themselves and fled to the west. Deas's advance was checked only by Sheridan's remaining brigades, Brigadier General William Lytle's and Colonel Nathan Walworth's (formerly Bradley's). Lytle's brigade especially made a strong stand on a ridge west of the Dyer Field. A noted poet from Cincinnati, Lytle had acquaintances among the senior leaders of both armies. Now, as he directed his brigade, he was struck by several bullets and killed. Outflanked and without their leader, Lytle's men also streamed westward down the ridge.

Hindman's left brigade, Brigadier General Arthur Manigault's, initially encountered little opposition as it crossed the large

ROSECRANS AND STAFF SURVEY A CONFEDERATE ASSAULT ON THEIR LINES AT CHICKAMAUGA.

(LC)

A CABIN STILL MARKS THE SITE OF THE SNODGRASS HOMESTEAD ON THE CHICKAMAUGA BATTLEFIELD.

(NPS)

field east of the Widow Glenn's. Manigault's right regiments participated in defeating Walworth's brigade, and his left units were on the verge of capturing the Glenn House when disaster struck. Quickly advancing from its reserve position four hundred yards to the southwest, Wilder's brigade struck Manigault's men a devastating blow. Aided by the Thirty-ninth Indiana Mounted Infantry, also armed with repeating rifles, Wilder sent Manigault's brigade reeling backward across the field. Wilder then cast about for additional targets. Just as he decided to attack the flank of Longstreet's penetration, Assistant Secretary of War Dana appeared. Dana excitedly announced that the battle was lost and demanded to be taken to Chattanooga. By the time Wilder was able to calm Dana and send him off with a small escort, the opportunity for offensive action had passed. Reluctantly, he ordered his men to withdraw westward.

Wilder's departure removed the last organized Federal unit from the southern half of the battlefield. Sheridan's and Davis's divisions had momentarily disintegrated and were fleeing with their commanders toward Missionary Ridge. Rosecrans himself was leaving the field, as were McCook and Crittenden. Each had attempted to rally broken units but had failed. McCook then chose an escape route that would eventually take him over Missionary Ridge into Chattanooga Valley. Rosecrans, Garfield, and others left the field via the road through McFarland's Gap. Near the gap Rosecrans and Garfield

MILITARY ARTIST JAMES WALKER INTERVIEWED PARTICIPANTS IN THE BATTLE AND VISITED THE FIELD BEFORE PAINTING THE FIGHTING AT SNODGRASS HILL. THE ACTION IS DEPICTED FROM A POSITION NORTHEAST OF THE SNODGRASS HOMESTEAD.

The Historiography of Chickamauga

The first detailed accounts of the Battle of Chickamauga appeared in newspapers published shortly after the conclusion of the action. Innacurate in many details, these hasty efforts nevertheless represented the first attempt to analyze the battle. In 1883 the story of Chickamauga assumed its modern form with the publication of *The Army of the Cumberland* by Henry Cist. A partisan staff officer of Rosecrans, Cist argued vigorously that the Federal defeat was primarily due to the incompetence of staff Major Frank Bond and the malevolence of Brigadier General Thomas Wood. Embellished over the years, Cist's analysis remains today the prevailing account of Chicamauga's pivotal events.

A decade later, Henry Boynton, another Rosecrans partisan and veteran of the battle, became the dominant member of the Chickamauga Park Commission. Like Rosecrans, Boynton maintained that Chickamauga had to be fought to secure Chattanooga, and thus was a Federal victory. While carefully locating many Federal markers, Boynton also skewed the interpretation of the field in favor of certain units, especially his own. The 1890 publication of Chickamauga battle reports in Volume XXX of the *War of the Rebellion: Official Records of the Union and Confederate Armies* notwithstanding, Cist's and Boynton's highly opinionated version of the battle was enshrined in the public mind by 1900.

Cist and Boynton had their detractors, notably maligned participants like Wood and veterans whose units had been slighted, but their objections were ignored. In 1911, Archibald Gracie, son of a Confederate participant, published *The Truth About Chickamauga.* Initially conceived as an effort to tell the Confederate side of the story, Gracie's work ultimately became an attack upon Boynton's placement of Federal units on Snodgrass Hill. Too narrow in scope and too technical in nature to have much of an impact on Chickamauga historiography, Gracie's book failed to produce a successful reinterpretation of the battle.

Since Gracie's time, many biographers have addressed Chickamauga as part of larger studies, often relying upon the Cist-Boynton versions in the process. Especially notable in this regard was William Lamers's 1961 biography of Rosecrans, *The Edge of Glory.* In the same year popular author Glenn Tucker published the first single-volume account of the Chickamauga Campaign in modern times. Filled with personal vignettes, Tucker's book relied heavily upon Cist's and Boynton's work but tempered some of their more partisan judgments. For the next thirty years, Tucker's *Chickamauga: Bloody Battle in the West* was the standard account of the battle.

Although scholarship has greatly improved since Tucker's day, many myths remain to be exorcised from the Chickamauga story. In 1971 Thomas Connelly resurrected the reputation of the Army of Tennessee in *Autumn of Glory* but continued the traditional bashing of Braxton Bragg. Fortunately, recent work by Judith Hallock and Steven Woodworth has finally begun to give Bragg his due. Some improvement has also been made on the Federal side, with the publication in 1992 of Peter Cozzens's *This Terrible Sound,* a full account of Chickamauga that has superseded Tucker's work. Still, as Cozzens's massive study proves, the Cist-Boynton version of events remains alive and well today.

Henry Van Ness Boynton

The Georgia Monument under construction in early 1899. The figure on top points the way to Chattanooga. (NPS)

paused, eventually deciding that Rosecrans would go to Chattanooga and prepare its defenses while Garfield tried to reach Thomas. Crittenden, meanwhile, also passed through McFarland's Gap. There he met Colonel John Parkhurst, provost marshal of the Fourteenth Corps, who had rallied more than a thousand fleeing soldiers. Offering them to Crittenden, Parkhurst was shocked when the corps commander refused the command and continued to the rear. Crittenden was not alone; everywhere men in blue uniforms hastened toward Chattanooga.

Unlike their commander, other soldiers of the Army of the Cumberland remained on the battlefield. Around the Kelly Field Thomas's four divisions still held their breastworks. On the ridge bending westward from the Snodgrass House a less organized but equally determined stand was made by men from many commands. First to reach the elevation later known as Snodgrass Hill or Horseshoe Ridge was Negley with Colonel William Sirwell's brigade. Negley had been on his way to join Thomas in late morning when a staff officer had brought him a verbal order to gather artillery on the ridge. Thomas wanted the artillery to cover his left flank, but the message was garbled or Negley, ill with diarrhea, misunderstood it. By the time Negley and Sirwell collected more than forty guns, the Confederate breakthrough had occurred. Soon hundreds of soldiers came pouring through the woods, many without organization or commanders. Mostly from Brannan's and Van Cleve's divisions, many demoralized men could not be rallied. Others decided to make a final stand on the ridge.

Arriving with the mob was Brannan, who attempted to bring order from the chaos. Asking Negley for assistance, Brannan received Sirwell's largest regiment, the Twenty-first Ohio. Armed with the five-shot Colt revolving rifle, the regiment anchored the right of the rallying fragments. Doubting that Brannan's rabble could stand for long, Negley decided to remove the artillery to McFarland's Gap. Not long after Negley departed, Stanley's brigade arrived, having been forced westward by Govan's attack. Although Stanley was soon wounded, his men occupied the section of ridge immediately south of the Snodgrass House. They were joined on their left by Harker's brigade, driven from the Dyer Field by Kershaw. In such fashion a new Federal line formed, not by conscious design but by the determination of hundreds of men to be driven no further. First to test that line was Kershaw's brigade. Several times Kershaw's regiments ascended the ridge, only to be beaten back by the concentrated fire of the defiant Federals. On Kershaw's right, Humphreys's brigade also approached the Federal line, but Humphreys deemed the Federal position too strong and held his men back.

GORDON GRANGER'S TIMELY ARRIVAL WITH PART OF THE UNION RESERVE CORPS, AS SHOWN IN THIS PAINTING BY HENRY A. OGDEN, PROVED AN IMMENSE RELIEF TO GENERAL THOMAS.

(COURTESY MICHAEL J. MCAFEE COLLECTION)

While Kershaw and Humphreys battled Brannan's and Wood's men on the eastern end of Horseshoe Ridge, Bushrod Johnson was ascending the western end

MID-AFTERNOON TO NIGHT, SUNDAY, SEPTEMBER 20, 1863

Union elements that survived the breakthrough form a defensive position on hills near the Snodgrass Farm and face mostly to the south. Despite repeated assaults, Confederates are not able to take the ridge until evening. Most of the Federal units have already withdrawn to Rossville and established defensive positions along Missionary Ridge.

At evening, Polk's wing renews its assault on the Kelly Farm defenses. The Union line at this end of the field is also pulling back, and the Confederates capture only a few hundred Federals.

The two Confederate wings will meet that night in what they would later call a triumphal celebration, but most of the Federal army had been able to withdraw in the direction of Chattanooga, contrary to Bragg's plan of September 16.

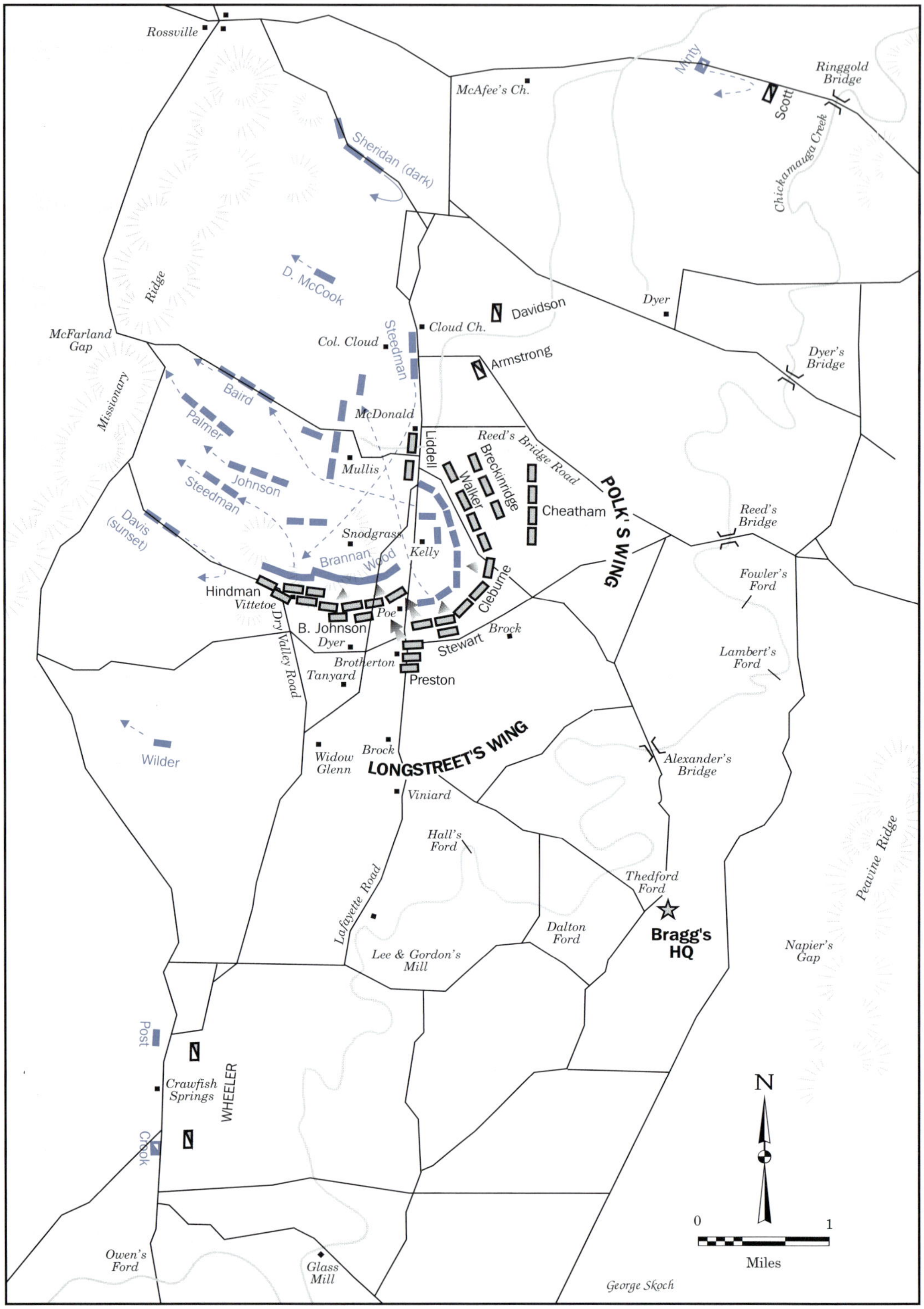

without opposition. After easily driving across the Dyer Field, Johnson had gained a ridge overlooking the Federal trains fleeing westward on the Dry Valley Road. For a time he contented himself with using his artillery to stampede the teamsters while his infantry rested. A little before 2:00 P.M. he turned his division northward toward Horseshoe Ridge. Climbing a spur on the western end of the wooded ridge, Johnson sensed that he was positioned on the flank of Federal troops facing Kershaw and Humphreys. Momentarily lacking McNair's (now Colonel David Coleman's) brigade, which was still reorganizing east of the Dyer Field, Johnson deployed Fulton's and Sugg's brigades before sending them toward the sounds of firing. As they reached the top of the main ridge they were surprised to meet a fresh Federal force climbing the opposite side.

The force that met Johnson consisted of two brigades of Brigadier General James Steedman's division of Granger's Reserve Corps. Originally posted at McAfee's Church east of Rossville, Granger and Steedman had listened all morning to the sounds of battle three miles to the south. At last, unable to restrain himself further, Granger ordered Steedman's two brigades and Colonel Daniel McCook's brigade to march to Thomas's aid. As they neared Thomas's flank they were harassed by some of Forrest's dismounted troopers. Deflected westward from the LaFayette Road by Forrest's artillery, Granger's men headed for the rear of the Federal position on Horseshoe Ridge. Leaving McCook's brigade north of the McDonald House to cover the rear, Granger and Steedman continued southwestward until they reached Thomas's beleaguered men. Ordered to prolong Brannan's line to the west, Granger sent Steedman's division into action on the run. With Brigadier General Walter Whitaker's brigade on the left and Colonel John Mitchell's brigade on the right, Steedman stormed up the hill into the teeth of Johnson's advance.

The shock of Steedman's attack caused Johnson's men to recoil down the hill. Following the retreating Confederates too closely, Steedman's men found themselves exposed and withdrew to the crest of the ridge. For the remainder of the afternoon the battle lines swayed back and forth across the top of the ridge as repeated Confederate assaults were repulsed, only to be renewed with greater effort. When Coleman's brigade finally appeared, Johnson threw it into his subsequent attack. In addition, his pleas for assistance resulted in Hindman's division being sent to add weight to his efforts. Deas's and Manigault's brigades formed on Fulton's left and participated in one charge but were so exhausted from their earlier exertions that they were useless thereafter.

For the remainder of the afternoon the battle lines swayed back and forth across the top of the ridge as repeated Confederate assaults were repulsed, only to be renewed with greater effort.

THE DIORAMA AT THE CHICKAMAUGA AND CHATTANOOGA NMP VISITOR CENTER DEPICTS THE NINTH OHIO INFANTRY CHARGING THE BRIGADE OF JOSEPH KERSHAW'S SOUTH CAROLINIANS ON THE SLOPES OF SNODGRASS HILL, SEPTEMBER 20, 1863. (NPS)

As Bragg dolefully rode away, Longstreet returned to the Dyer Field. There he finally began to impose some central direction upon the disjointed Confederate assaults futilely smashing themselves against the ridge.

Similarly, Anderson's Brigade filled the gap between Johnson and Kershaw and made its own unsuccessful assault against the hill. Obviously, Johnson's and Hindman's men no longer had the offensive punch needed to carry the commanding Federal position, especially after Van Derveer's brigade arrived from Kelly Field to strengthen the defense.

For some time the developing fight for Horseshoe Ridge did not gain Longstreet's attention. After the initial breakthrough he visited his right flank at the Poe Field, ordered Buckner to deploy more artillery, then sat down to a convivial lunch with his staff. Summoned by Bragg, he asked for reinforcements even though he had not yet committed his own reserve, Preston's division. Depressed that another victory was slipping from his grasp, Bragg claimed that Polk's right wing was too badly hurt to provide assistance. As Bragg dolefully rode away, Longstreet returned to the Dyer Field. There he finally began to impose some central direction upon the disjointed Confederate assaults futilely smashing themselves against the ridge. Missing since Hood had been carried from the field, that central direction could possibly have swept the haggard Federal defenders from their fiery Gibraltar before nightfall. Now Longstreet would have to race the sun as well as defeat the enemy. With only one last unit to deploy, he called Preston's division forward.

Around 4:30 P.M. Brigadier General Archibald Gracie's brigade reached the foot of Horseshoe Ridge. Taken under fire instantly, Gracie's troops began the first of several attempts to seize the eastern end of the ridge. On their left, Colonel John Kelly's brigade joined the assaults, with similar lack of success. By the time Colonel Robert Trigg's brigade arrived on Kelly's left, Gracie's and Kelly's men had lost their momentum. Gracie had gained the edge of the first knoll southwest of the Snodgrass House but could go no further, while Kelly was still at the foot of the ridge. With Trigg's fresh regiments at hand, Preston decided to make one last effort before darkness enveloped the field. Sensing a slackening of Federal fire on his left, he sent Trigg up a ravine in hopes of flanking the troops facing Kelly. Without opposition, the brigade crossed the ridge, then

SKETCH OF HORSES AND CAISSONS ON THE FIELD AFTER THE BATTLE.

(*SOLDIER IN OUR CIVIL WAR*)

turned eastward. In the gloom Trigg's and Kelly's brigades encircled remnants of three Federal regiments. Except for the wounded and the dead, these regiments were the last Federals on Horseshoe Ridge. Where had the remainder of the Army of the Cumberland gone?

Around 4:30 P.M., in response to an order from Rosecrans, Thomas ordered a general retreat, beginning with the four divisions holding Kelly Field. Reynolds's division began the delicate movement, with Turchin's brigade in the lead. Finding skirmishers of Liddell's division blocking the way, Turchin led a wild charge which brushed them aside and cleared the McFarland's Gap Road. After Reynolds, it was Palmer's turn to go. Having already sent Hazen's brigade to Horseshoe Ridge, Palmer extracted his remaining two brigades with increasing difficulty. Seeing the retreat, the Confederates redoubled their attacks against the Federal position. As Johnson's and Baird's units struggled to disengage, Stewart's, Cleburne's, and even some of Cheatham's men closed in around them. Johnson's three brigades escaped relatively intact, but Baird lost heavily, especially in prisoners. Leaping the works, the Confederate infantrymen raised a victory shout that was heard far to the east, where Bragg was sitting disconsolately on a log.

Before leaving Horseshoe Ridge, Thomas placed Granger in charge of the defense, but Granger remained only a little longer than Thomas. When he departed, no one coordinated the Federal withdrawal from the ridge. As sunset approached, Steedman disengaged his division and quietly withdrew to the north without being noticed by Bushrod Johnson or Hindman. Similarly, Brannan and Wood managed the withdrawal of their troops without reference to Steedman's departure. Left behind in the center of the position were three regiments, all of which had been temporarily attached to either Steedman or Brannan. The Twenty-second Michigan and the Eighty-ninth Ohio regiments had entered the fight with Whitaker's brigade and had been ordered to remain in place by one of Steedman's staff officers. The Twenty-first Ohio regiment had been given to Brannan by Negley early in the afternoon. It too was told by persons seemingly in authority

UNION WOUNDED FROM CHICKAMAUGA ARRIVING AT STEVENSON, ALABAMA, ON SEPTEMBER 23, 1863. SKETCH BY J.F.C. HILLEN FROM *FRANK LESLIE'S ILLUSTRATED NEWSPAPER.*

...the Army of the Cumberland appeared to be evacuating Chattanooga. Bragg therefore ordered a pause to reorganize his shattered units and gather the spoils of war, which lay everywhere on the field.

to hold its position with the bayonet. Decimated by casualties and out of ammunition, the three regiments heroically held their position until surrounded and captured by Preston's Division.

As darkness shrouded the battlefield of Chickamauga, few on either side were aware that the struggle had ended. During the night Thomas withdrew his intact units to positions around Rossville Gap and across Chattanooga Valley. Behind this new line broken units reconstituted themselves. Unaware that the Army of the Cumberland was gone, the Army of Tennessee bivouacked where they lay, expecting to renew the contest on the following day. Only gradually did the Confederate commanders realize that they held the field alone. Immediate pursuit was tempting, but practical considerations ruled it out. Bragg's army had lost more than 17,000 men killed, wounded, and missing. Many of the troops that had arrived by rail had brought no transportation with them, and the battle had seriously depleted the number of serviceable artillery horses. There was no pontoon train available for crossing the Tennessee River. Besides, the Army of the Cumberland appeared to be evacuating Chattanooga. Bragg therefore ordered a pause to reorganize his shattered units and gather the spoils of war, which lay everywhere on the field.

Holding Missionary Ridge only long enough to regain its composure, the Army of the Cumberland soon withdrew into Chattanooga. Rosecrans's command was badly hurt, having lost more than 16,000 men killed, wounded, and missing in the battle. Many of the wounded had been left to the Confederates, either on the battlefield or at field hospitals that could not be evacuated. Although the army had saved most of its trains, large quantities of arms, ammunition, and matériel had been left behind. Nevertheless, most of the men were not demoralized and still retained confidence in Rosecrans. Using old Confederate works as a foundation, engineers quickly designed a strong defensive line. Digging with great energy, the Army of the Cumberland soon felt secure from a frontal attack. Its supply situation was much more tenuous because the Confederates controlled the easiest routes to the Stevenson supply base. Still, as long as Chattanooga remained in Federal hands, both Rosecrans and the Army of the Cumberland could truthfully claim that the objective of the campaign had been attained. Similarly, for Bragg and the Army of Tennessee, as long as they were denied possession of Chattanooga the great victory of Chickamauga would remain incomplete. Clearly, the iron hand of war had not yet finished its work in the shadow of Lookout Mountain.